The Tortoise U

The Tortoise Usually Wins

Biblical Reflections on Quiet Leadership For Reluctant Leaders

Brian Harris

Paternoster:
thinking faith

20 19 18 17 16 15 14   8 7 6 5 4 3 2

First published 2013 by Paternoster
Reprinted 2014
Paternoster is an imprint of Authentic Media Limited
52 Presley Way, Crownhill, Milton Keynes, MK8 0ES.
www.authenticmedia.co.uk

British Library Cataloguing in Publication Data

A catalogue record for this book is available from the British Library

ISBN 978-1-84227-787-4
978-1-78078-302-4 (e-book)

Cover Design by David McNeill (www.revocreative.co.uk)
Printed and bound by CPI Group (UK) Ltd., Croydon, CR0 4YY

Dedicated to my mother, Anne Patricia Harris
1926–2012

Contents

Contents

Contents

Contents

Contents

Foreword

Some years ago I was struck by George Barna's guestimate about the two main kinds of leadership that he published in *A Fish Out of Water* (2002). Based on twenty years of leadership research he claimed that only one out of every eight individuals is a natural-born leader. He calls these 'habitual leaders' with leadership qualities in their DNA. In contrast, the vast majority of us are 'situational leaders' who lack instinctual leadership qualities and flair yet find ourselves in circumstances where leadership becomes unavoidable. Inevitably the difference between five-star born leaders and one-star enforced leaders shows up dramatically in terms of confidence levels and skills. On one hand self-confident leaders know what to do and command respect, while on the other hand reluctant leaders may resign themselves to muddle along. Barna wrote to encourage the tens of millions of situational leaders that we can be useful for God and are capable of developing enough skills to direct vision for our particular (and limited) contexts. But I couldn't escape the notion that situational leaders are really rather second-rate and at best can only hope to adopt some of the skills that are instinctive to habitual leaders. Frankly, that is how the secular world largely views leadership, rating highly those who demonstrate dazzling leadership qualities and dismissing the plodders. Yes, habitual leaders are more prone to self-confidence, arrogance and egotism but that is assumed to go with the territory of highly prized leadership.

Thoughtfully, Brian Harris confronts this secular assumption and dramatically raises the worth of situational leaders, whom he calls 'quiet leaders'. He understands well the difficulties that seven-eighths of us meet when we are faced with leadership responsibilities and, like Barna, he emphasizes the need to be realistic and intentional in working through the implications of leadership. With imagination (as with Myrtle the tortoise!) he gives excellent practical advice throughout the book, with insightful use of wide-ranging leadership material and helpful interviews grounding key issues at the conclusion of each chapter.

But what I found especially exhilarating was the biblical elevation of 'quiet leadership' grounded in the key images of servant, shepherd and steward. Deftly he draws out implications for quiet leadership's spiritual power, especially employing a framework of virtue ethics with relevant values. And what values! Modesty, restraint, tenacity, interdependence and other-centredness. When did you last see those stressed in leadership literature? As I read on through Brian's book, it hit me how strongly positioned quiet leaders are to model these qualities. Indeed, because of their reduced expectations of their personal leadership qualities, quiet leaders are far more likely to model Christ's way than heroic leaders whose large egos have much greater difficulty engaging with such biblical understanding of spiritual leadership. Far from allowing the notion that quiet leaders are inferior and must somehow grasp some principles that are second nature to genuine leaders, here we see quiet leaders are closer to expressing Christian leadership.

It is a supreme Christian leadership paradox that the world's strongest personality, Jesus Christ, actually models 'quiet leadership' with virtues and values unlike the world has ever seen. Who else has shown restraint, tenacity and other-centredness like him? Before a watching world that has always admired heroic leaders, he models a new way of leadership by washing his disciples' dirty feet (John 13:1–17). John Adair, in *Inspiring Leaders*, claims that this event is the most extraordinary scene in the history of leadership. Without a doubt, Jesus Christ stands at the head of the world's one-eighth habitual leaders who have spiritual leadership in their DNA. Yet, he demonstrates such qualities of quiet leadership that paradoxically lie more easily within reach of those who are situational leaders.

Recently I preached on 'Blessed are the meek, for they will inherit the earth' (Matt. 5:5), and I pleaded that we rescue the word 'meekness'. Nobody wants to be described as 'meek' because it is associated with words like 'mild' and 'weak'. Yet, this key word which describes Moses in the Old Testament (Num. 12:3) proves to be a vital word for Jesus Christ (Matt. 11:28). Meekness is 'gentleness with the strength of steel'. It is strength of personality under God's control! It demonstrates such virtues as modesty, restraint, tenacity, interdependence and other-centredness. After the sermon someone commented to me that this beatitude is the most counter-cultural of them all. It declares that this combination of Christ-like qualities will ultimately inherit the earth! It may not look to the world as though meekness can possibly lead to success but this is God's way. Extraordinary.

I was reminded of this comment as I read through this delight-fully written and practically oriented book. Quiet leaders are in the majority and God made us that way. But how much he can use us for his kingdom when, with modesty, realism and intention-ality, we commit ourselves to lead for him.

Michael Quicke
CW Koller Professor of Preaching
Northern Seminary, Lombard, USA

Preface

Some people seem born to lead. It is hard to dispute this. Observe the playground of your local kindergarten and you will quickly pick those kids who delight in taking charge of situations. Without consciously thinking about it, they decide which game will be played, who will be included and the role each will fulfil. Their lives often reflect a comparable trajectory, as time and again they find themselves surrounded by enthusiastic followers, happily travelling in the same direction.

This book is not written for such people. Of course, they are welcome to read it, and who knows, they might glean a pearl of wisdom here and there, but something inside of them will be saying, 'I'm not really a leader like that. I'm sure leadership is a lot more spontaneous than that.' And for them it is. I bear such leaders no malice. To the contrary, I delight in their giftedness, assurance and confidence in leadership. It is just that I have not written this book for them.

The leaders I had in mind, as I worked away at the keyboard while on sabbatical from Vose Seminary and serving as a visiting professor at Carson Newman, are a different breed. They are reluctant leaders. They often wish they could hand the mantle of leadership over to someone else and, if a suitable opportunity arose, they probably would. They might not be sure how they landed up in a position of leadership, and wonder if they have what it takes. But they are willing to give it a go. They would like a little help as they travel in unfamiliar territory, and while they understand that trite formulas don't work, they are open and willing to learn. But they are sure of one thing. If they are suddenly told that they have to become superhuman, heroic leaders, they will put the book to one side and gloomily reflect that it is just not going to happen.

If I have targeted reluctant leaders it is because I have noticed a breed of leaders who make a significant difference to their organization, yet they do it quietly. Their success is linked more to their persistence, tenacity and flexibility than to their charisma. While the latter is sometimes present, it is often not. These are the leaders you don't necessarily notice at dinner parties, and you certainly wouldn't pick them out in a supermarket line, yet day after day they go about making a difference.

I first noticed it when I reflected on the impact of the ministry of several pastors I know. Some are in the charismatic leader category, and it was not hard to figure out why they have been successful. But several were not. Indeed, some of them seem dour and hesitant. But their track record of successful ministry is beyond dispute. Time and again they have gone into difficult situations and turned them around. Success did not come overnight, but it certainly came. No doubt the work of God's Spirit had a fair amount to do with it, but God always works with people, and uses what they offer. And I noticed that these quieter leaders often offer similar things. They remind me of Aesop's story of the tortoise and the hare. There is no mistaking that they are aligned to the tortoise. Steady plodders, knowing the route they need to go, keeping at it in spite of the odds, and declining the seductive detours that the hare finds irresistible, they make it across the finishing line, and do so time and time again. I was intrigued, and so began my study of quiet leadership.

I am more convinced than ever that while for a small minority leadership comes spontaneously and easily, it is within the grasp of a far larger number of people. Indeed, leadership is not magical. It is about knowing that something matters, and that you need to help a group attain it. If the only way they will get there is if you do the leading, so be it, lead. When we break leadership down into the component parts, it is a step-at-a-time process. And this book tries to walk through some of the more important steps.

The opening chapter surveys the theory of quiet leadership. It asks and answers why the tortoise usually wins, realizing that Aesop's fable, birthed thousands of years ago, highlights a fundamental truth – the race is often not won by the fastest but by the most persistent. Those who stay the course cross the finish line.

The second chapter explores the theology of quiet leadership. It notes that three recurring biblical images of leadership, namely the leader as servant, shepherd and steward, have little to do with heroic conceptions of leadership. To the contrary, they move in a different direction. They are disturbing images because they have nothing to do with gloss and glamour. Their focus is on the other – those served by our leadership, a corrective that is often desperately needed.

Leaders have to make decisions and decisions have ethical repercussions. The third chapter provides some tools to help in the process of making morally satisfying decisions. It doesn't offer foolproof solutions, but gives enough pointers to enhance the likelihood of the right questions being asked and grappled with. It is supplemented with an intriguing case-study of the Hebrew midwives, Shiphrah and Puah, who faced an impossible quandary after being ordered by the Pharaoh of their day to execute all male Hebrew babies at birth. Their morally messy solution has much to teach us – especially as God gave it the thumbs up, which teaches us a great deal about the ethical heartbeat of God.

No two leadership journeys are exactly the same, and nor should they be. A key step in leadership is to find our particular leadership voice, and Chapter 4 explores some key dimensions in this.

The remaining chapters adopt a step-by-step approach to leadership. There is nothing flashy in what they suggest. Quiet leaders know that there are certain things that need to be done. If we can't lead our own self, our leadership journey is likely to be brief, so Chapter 5 explores the importance of challenging our excuses and embarking on a journey of growth and development.

Chapter 6 explores the realm of results and keeping an eye on outputs, and how to enhance them. Naturally we need to be sure the results we cite are ones that we hoped to attain. For that we need a vision of where we should go. Casting vision is a key leadership task, and Chapter 7 discusses attainable ways to do so.

Quiet leaders are not in leadership for their own ego. Because they are servant leaders, they are concerned about what happens to those who follow their lead. Chapter 8, 'What Others Become', delves into the area of helping others to shine and suggests ways to bring the best out of those who take the risk of following our lead.

When things go right, it is usually as a result of leaderships (plural) rather than leadership (singular). Quiet leaders know this. Their temperament is such that they would be alarmed at the prospect of everything depending upon them. True, at times they have to be willing to go it alone, but their instinct is to work with others and to include others in the process. To do so successfully involves learning to work effectively with teams. Chapter 9 dives into this fascinating arena.

There are all kinds of practical things that leaders need to do. Time management, running effective meetings, delegation and conflict resolution are bread-and-butter issues for all leaders. Hopefully the insights discussed in Chapter 10 will lead to better outcomes.

I hope you will be able to earth this book in the reality of your own setting. Perhaps you are already a leader, or you might sense that leadership is something that might come your way. You might aspire to leadership not because you wish to be a leader, but because you know that the present status quo cannot continue and that someone must rise to the challenge. You sense that there is no compelling reason why that person should not be you. I have tried to earth each topic by interviewing an effective quiet leader at the end of each chapter. I am hugely in their debt. Each has impacted my own leadership in some way, and I imagine that their insights will be helpful for you as well. Each interview is followed by questions for reflection. You might choose to do that on your own or, better still, with a few others. It is so much better to be part of a team of quiet leaders than to be a quiet leader on your own. Perhaps the group discussion will inspire others to join the tortoise in getting to the finish line ahead of the hare.

The closing chapter tells the tale of the difference made by some quiet leaders in my part of the world, Perth, Australia. In an age where church denominations are in rapid decline, why has the Baptist Union of Western Australia grown so rapidly? True, Perth is growing quickly, but the growth of the denomination has significantly outstripped the population growth. Sadly that does not happen in many parts of the Western world. It is a quiet leadership story waiting to be told. And then there is the remarkable ministry of Carey – a church, school and community service organization in Perth. It was birthed by a youthful group of twenty-somethings, and yet has an astonishing impact. It is another quiet leadership story that should fill you with hopefulness for your own setting.

I have so many people to thank for the success of this project.

To the team at Vose Seminary where I am truly privileged to serve as principal – thank you. They constantly cover for my leadership flaws and together we've been able to birth an innovative seminary that punches above its weight over and over again. It is so much fun to be there. Needless to say, we also have the world's best students, and I say that because it is true, and to acknowledge my debt to them.

To the staff at Carey, who provide a second context in which I am able to exercise quiet leadership, thank you. They always go the second mile in ways that delight and surprise. Special thanks to Sue Gifford for her help with questions of design.

Carson Newman College, Tennessee, provided an ideal location in which I could write the bulk of this book. I am especially indebted to David Crutchley and his staff for their support and encouragement, and to the college president, Randall O'Brien, for his insight and wisdom.

And there are so many others. Wayne Belcher read and re read the manuscript for me, making many helpful suggestions. The staff at Paternoster, and especially Dr Michael Parsons, have been exceptionally helpful. I am delighted to serve as part of the executive team of the Baptist Union of Western Australia, and owe each member of that team a great deal. They have taught me much about leadership. And my family has been encouraging and supportive, as they always are. Somehow we manage to have enormous fun in the midst of a crowded schedule, and that owes much to their creativity and flexibility.

I have dedicated this book to my mother. Sadly she died shortly before I finished it. During her eighty-six years on this planet she touched the lives of many people with her gentle kindness, acceptance and encouragement. Her faith was genuine, deep and winsome. A pharmacist by profession and calling, she turned the pharmacy where she served for over thirty years into a vibrant centre for community and, in doing so, enriched the lives of many.

Preface

She gave me roots that are so deep that I have always been free to fly. I miss her terribly, but salute her as a wonderful quiet leader who made a difference.

Brian Harris
Vose Seminary, Perth, Australia
September 2012

The Tortoise Usually Wins:
The Theory of Quiet Leadership

I have seen something else under the sun: The race is not to the swift
or the battle to the strong, nor does food come to the wise or wealth to
the brilliant or favour to the learned; but time and chance happen to
them all – Ecclesiastes 9:11

About Myrtle

You probably know Aesop's fable of the tortoise and the hare.
Unlikely competitors in a race, it is obvious who the favourite is.
The hare is faster, shrewder and considerably more charismatic.
But in the fable, the tortoise lands up winning. Seems that the
hare, so confident of his prowess, took some time off for a nap.
The challenge didn't seem great enough for him and victory was
always assured. By contrast the tortoise, fully aware of his limitations, kept plodding along, and against the odds, crossed the
finishing line first.

Is this a fable for our time?

Let's explore it. Why does the tortoise win?

First thing that springs to mind is that he (or perhaps it was
she, who knows with tortoises?) refused to face the obvious. The
hare was far faster and better endowed. Even a cursory glance at
the differences between them was enough to persuade the boldest
heart that this was a day best to be spent in bed. By refusing to be
intimidated by obstacles, the hero of this tale demonstrates why
he (or she) was victorious. Let's face it, very few things that are

worth achieving don't have some obstacles in the way. If their existence sees us hand in our resignation letter, the likelihood of our ever succeeding is extremely slight.

Second, our tortoise kept on doing what she knew best. Putting one foot in front of the other is not newsworthy, especially when the length of each stride is restricted by a rather cumbersome shell, but each small step in the same direction adds up. In the end the finishing line was not only in sight, but crossed. Tenacity and endurance are key factors in success. With them, we will usually make progress. Without them, we quickly undo any progress we previously made.

Third, she was fortunate enough to have a lazy opponent! Not all factors in life are under our control, and at times the coincidental works for us, at other times, against us. This is not to say that the tortoise didn't make a shrewd guess at the hare's lack of stickability. Wise leaders usually take into account how much the other team wants to win. Sometimes victory goes not to those who could most easily attain it, but to those who desire it the most.

While I love this fable, it has its limitations. In the end it's about a lone tortoise beating a gifted but complacent hare. Trouble is, not all hares are complacent, and when they aren't, they leave your average tortoise in the dust. In fact, even a partially motivated hare is likely to cross the finish line well ahead of any member of the turtle clan.

So is there any hope for your average plodder when the highly talented opposition is even half alert? Well, put yourself in our tortoise's (we'll call her Myrtle from now on) position.

Myrtle could simply have put the contest into the too-hard box. Knowing the right league to play in is important. I used to be a pretty average squash player – on my better days, a little above average. Inadvertently I once challenged a former national player to a game. It wasn't fun for either of us. True, I claimed the occasional point along the way, but they were few and far between. There was no tortoise versus hare upset result. The bottom line is simple; if we're going to leap a few leagues ahead of ourselves we need to have thought through our strategy in advance. So given that Myrtle wanted to take part in the race, what options were open?

One fairly obvious route would have been to get in a little extra help. While Aesop doesn't fill us in on the rules of this race, given that the hare was allowed to take time out for a nap, we can assume that they weren't written up too tightly. Getting a little help along the way is a key strategy for quiet leaders. They know they can't do it all, so develop enough emotional intelligence to be able to win the allegiance of others.

Linked to this point, the best quiet leaders think in terms of leaderships (plural) rather than leadership (singular). The strong, silent, lone-ranger-style leader might win our awe by their talent and ability, but when you are built like Myrtle, you know that only a team effort will get you across the line.

There is also one other option and, truth to tell, this is my favourite. Perhaps the finish line was en route for Myrtle. Being in the direction she was already heading, it is possible she didn't mind if the hare raced alongside and helped her set a slightly faster pace than might otherwise have been the case. Perhaps (and Aesop has been dead far too long to contradict me!) Myrtle thought she had nothing to lose. After all, she was heading in that direction anyway, her participation was likely to see her get there a little faster, and as no one expected her to win, at worst she would meet expectations. And of course there was the tiny possibility that the other competitor would have a nap along the way. In this instance, as in life, long odds sometimes come off, so why not take them when you have nothing to lose?

So why is this option my favourite? Well, as a quiet leader I'm convinced that the best journeys aren't undertaken to defeat someone else, but because they are the journey we want to undertake. If there is a little competition along the way, so be it – but it is best when that is not the motivator, else we could find ourselves doing things to prove a point rather than focusing on what really matters to us.

We could keep speculating about this intriguing race, but let's move to our topic of quiet leadership a little more systematically.

I've written this book for those who consider themselves as unlikely leaders. If you are one of them, you probably don't consider yourself to be the most talented, charismatic or gifted individual. You might have landed up in a leadership position, but are perhaps surprised that you got there. Alternatively, you might be well aware that you gained the post because you were the only available candidate. Or it could be that you hold no leadership position, but you'd like to, not because you relish the limelight, but because you believe in what your group is trying to do and you'd really like to help them to do it a little better. It could even be that the thought of leadership makes you want to run a mile, but you feel disgruntled with the way things are and wish that there were better leaders around to deal with the challenge. It could be that your name is written against that challenge, even though that option hadn't previously dawned on you and the thought of it fills you with an uneasy sense of panic.

All these scenarios are ones that call for quiet leadership.

Quiet leadership is a theory of leadership that sidesteps questions of charisma, and when looking at the characteristics of a leader focuses on leadership virtues and values, rather than innate abilities. It explores ways to have influence regardless of formal position, and it examines the relationship between desired outcomes and virtues such as restraint, modesty and tenacity.

It debunks the myth that the good is the enemy of the best and suggests that the reverse is true. Too often competent people are paralyzed into inactivity by unattainable images of perfection. Rather than make their helpful contribution, they retreat so as not to be in the way of a great leader. The trouble is that very few great leaders exist. While it is wonderful when they do, the leadership void in most organizations points to their rarity. Quiet leaders realize this. They are modest enough to know they are not great, but they are tenacious and committed to the task and willing to work co-operatively with others to achieve it. When released to make their good contribution, very pleasing things happen. What's more they happen in real life – not in the fantasy land of non-existent heroes.

In justifying his focus on quiet leadership, one of its key advocates, Joseph Badaracco, writes: 'over the course of a career spent studying management and leadership, I have observed that the most effective leaders are rarely public heroes. These men and women are rarely high profile champions . . . They move patiently, carefully, and incrementally.'[1]

A little later he writes: 'I have come to call these people quiet leaders because their modesty and restraint are in large measure responsible for their impressive achievements. And since big problems can only be resolved by a long series of small efforts, quiet leadership, despite its seemingly slow pace, often turns out to be the quickest way to make an organization – and the world – a better place.'[2]

Quiet leaders are realists. It doesn't mean that they lack idealism, but they are conscious of their starting point. In the tortoise and hare fable, Myrtle is under no illusion as to her speed. She is aware that the journey to the finish line is made by tenaciously putting one foot in front of the other, and that she does not have enough charisma to allow deviation from that path. It is not a glamorous plan, but it gets her to the finish line ahead of the hare.

To some extent the theory of quiet leadership is counterintuitive to what we seem to value at present. This is the age of the cult of personality. Those we most admire are larger-than-life figures. They are never stumped for words and, unlike us, are at ease in all social situations. They are smarter, wealthier, fitter and more beautiful than we can ever hope to be. The work they do seems so much more important than the modest fare that fills our daily agenda. They are leaders and therefore, clearly, we are not.

In spite of the popularity of such views, they represent a tired and stereotypical view of leadership. They owe their origin to the belief that leaders are born, not made, and that you've therefore either got it, or not. They focus on leaders rather than on leadership, usually falsely assuming that the two are synonymous. And they forget that sometimes persistent tortoise-like plodding in the same direction produces dividends larger than would usually be imagined.

Some theories of leadership

Though there are many different views about leadership, most views fall roughly within at least one or two of the following four views of leadership:

- View 1 emphasizes the characteristics of a leader, noting special qualities that those who lead tend to have in common. Oft-cited *characteristics* include charisma, commitment, courage, focus, self-discipline, a positive attitude and vision.[3] It is sometimes known as the 'heroic' view of leadership, because the leader has to be something of a hero to perform all the tasks expected of them.

- View 2 focuses on *position*. The leader is the one who holds a certain position. Thus a school principal is the CEO of the school, and presumably its leader. It is the old military concept that you respect and obey the rank rather than the person. Of course this sidesteps the question of how the person came to gain the rank in the first place. It can also be argued that 'position is simply a context for leadership'.[4]

- View 3 places the emphasis on *influence*. Leaders shape the thinking and actions of others. In this view, if you want to know if you are a leader, look behind you. If no one is following, then you're presumably not a leader because you aren't influencing others. The influence the quiet leader might have is not always obvious if you only look to the person who stands at the front of the stage. Quiet leaders often influence others by getting alongside them. Thoughtful one-on-one conversations or chatting with small groups is often the bread-and-butter work of a quiet leader as they gain influence.

- View 4, which in some respects overlaps with view 3, focuses on *outcomes*. When leaders are around, things happen. It might not be immediately obvious why, but after a while you notice a pattern. The presence of some people leads to constructive change . . . and it happens over and over again. There is a subtle difference between views 3 and 4. View 4 adds an additional requirement to view 3. Some people are able to influence other people, but because they have never thought about where they would like to go, their influence has few, if any, positive outcomes. Some influential people waste their leadership opportunity by persuading those who look to them to be as discontented as they are. Sometimes their legacy is that they have used their influence to ensure that people do nothing, or that nothing in their organization changes. Views of leadership that focus on outcomes insist that leaders not only be able to influence others, but they intentionally use that influence to aim for a desired outcome.

We don't need to choose between these different perspectives.[5] Each has a measure of truth, and they usually interact. Position is most often gained because of demonstrated characteristics and influence. However, this is not always the case. Sometimes people lack a formal position but have huge influence. At other times people have a position that one would assume gives influence, but in practice might have very little influence and only minimally impact outcomes.

Those who lead lives that are a little more remarkable have usually been able to maximize the potential they have in each of the four areas of characteristics, position, influence and outcomes, while at the same time they work to reduce any shortfall between the potential that exists in each of these areas, and what is actually being achieved. Remember the hare. No one doubted his ability, but when it came to the contest he performed way below his potential. The journey from possibility to actuality is often the longest of all. Quiet leaders are realistic about this and are not disheartened when all dreams are not realized overnight.

A little self-analysis can be helpful. Figures 1.1, 1.2, 1.3 and 1.4 explore the leadership potential we have as the result of our position or character or influence or outcomes, against the actual reality of the situation. Where would you plot yourself on each of these graphs? Spend a little time grappling with the question. If there is a significant gap between potential and actuality, keep asking why until you come up with some answers that can be acted upon.

Let's work with an example to make the exercise more concrete. Figure 1.1 shows how hypothetical Amy, newly appointed as a head of department at the school she has been teaching at for the last seven years, plots herself . . .

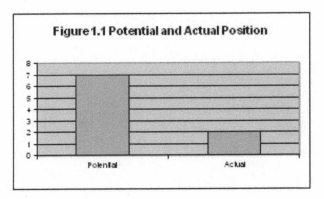

7

Comment on Figure 1.1: Amy has got into a leadership position that could open many doors of opportunity, but as of yet, these are not being realized. As she is very new to the position, it could be that she is struggling to make the change from her previous 'regular staff member' status to that of head of department, or that the school is structured in such a way that titular leaders don't have the power one would anticipate (in which case the potential might be lower than one would have imagined) or that . . . why don't you fill in some options?

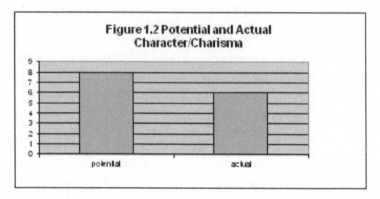

Comment on Figure 1.2: There is not much gap between the two, so Amy is currently using her charisma and natural gifting to aid her leadership. This is not always the case. For example, some people are hugely gifted but are in positions that allow little scope for their gifting to grow. Leaders should look out for such people and think of ways to ensure that new doors of opportunity open for them.

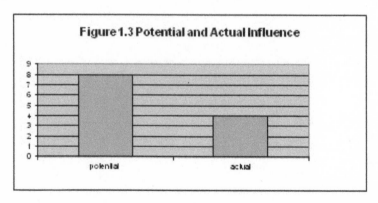

Comment on Figure 1.3: Amy is in a position to influence many people, but is currently only partly achieving this potential. A reason could be that she doesn't yet realize how much influence she can potentially have . . . or she might shy away from it.

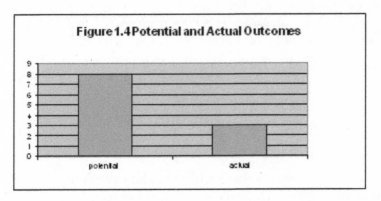

Comment on Figure 1.4: Amy is in a position where outcomes could be significant. At this stage, they are not being realized. Sometimes outcomes take a little longer. Often people need to think more carefully through what the desired outcomes should be and start to work more consistently towards them.

A task: Do this exercise for yourself. How do you rank yourself in terms of your potential for leadership as a result of your position, character/charisma, influence or the outcomes you are achieving – and then where do you rank yourself in terms of what you are actually achieving as a result of each? Is there a gap between your potential and the current reality? If there is, ask yourself why. What can you do about it?

We started this chapter by asking why the tortoise wins. We could have asked, why does the hare lose? It's just as important a question. We could put it down to laziness, or failing to take the race seriously, or over-confidence, or not having his heart fully in what he was doing. In the hare's case, all of these options are probably true. In their own way it is only right that they should serve as warnings to us.

Why many give up . . .

There are other common reasons why some leaders give up. In a fascinating study of why many run away from leadership, Dan Allender suggests that there are five challenges that all leaders eventually face – and often it is by tomorrow![6]

Let's quickly rattle off the list before exploring it:

1. Crisis
2. Complexity
3. Betrayal
4. Loneliness
5. Weariness

Allender supplements these with what he calls faulty or ineffectual responses to each challenge (cowardice, rigidity, narcissism, hiding and fatalism) and then more hopefully offers effective responses to them (courage, depth, gratitude, openness, hope).

So let us explore the list.

Crisis

Crises happen. The awkward thing about a crisis is that when it happens, eyes tend to gravitate towards the leader. While forward planning, good time management and contingency plans are always helpful when a crisis strikes, even the best leaders are sometimes confronted with the unexpected. To reflect on our opening quote from the Bible, the race is often not to the swift or to the wise because, as the sage of old noted, time and chance happen to us all (Eccl. 9:11). Even if you've planned what you will do if a fire destroys your workplace, you're dreaming if you think that your plans will prevent it from being a setback.

Crisis periods are often the time when quiet leaders shine. It's a head down, keep going, don't panic period. By being unflappable, quiet leaders reassure those who are anxious. There are times when strong up-front leadership is needed during a crisis, but it's not charismatic rhetoric that is looked for. It is openness, honesty, transparency about the issues faced – and all of this bathed in a gentle, but not naïve, optimism. Often the most important factor in being able to overcome a crisis is the leader's willingness to front up and to make it clear that the issue is being treated seriously.

Complexity

While we have a deep-seated love of lists that are three to five points long and which will solve whatever issue we face, such lists rarely work. The concerns we face are often very complex. Weaker leaders try to avoid complexity by pretending it doesn't exist. They sometimes caricature alternate responses and try to make their argument look stronger by ridiculing those who take a different perspective. Such an approach is deeply divisive, and often results in difficult decisions being implemented with the maximum amount of pain.

Quiet leaders are fully aware of and respectful of alternate points of view. They realize that an organization cannot vacillate between decisions, and that a key leadership responsibility is that of making decisions, even when the issue is complex. They are willing to consult, discuss and negotiate – but in the end they recognize that a decision must be made. Conscious that an alternate decision could have been made, they are respectful of those who would have preferred the alternative, while being willing to articulate the reasons for taking the decision made. Managing complexity in this way is far more likely to achieve a helpful outcome.

In working with complexity, I've found the concept of embracing paradox, or colliding truths, to be liberating. A paradox is something that involves an inherent contradiction. It consists of two propositions that are both essentially true but that appear to contradict each other. Rather than trying to find (or reject) a middle path of balance we are often called to live with the legitimacy of various perspectives and options. Maloney elaborates on this when he writes about moving from an 'or' to an 'and' style of leadership.[7]

A common colliding truth that leaders face is the person/organization paradox.

With the best will in the world, the quiet leader sometimes has to acknowledge that the needs of an employee are not the same as the needs of the company. Perhaps an employee has been appointed to a position to which they are less suited than first appeared to be the case. They might have resigned from another post because of the challenge and opportunity the new job offered. The bridges back might have been burnt. In spite of additional training and mentoring, the person isn't able to perform the job to the standard required. The probationary period may be drawing to a close. Does the quiet leader terminate the person's employment knowing that this is in the best interest of the company, or should they hold on to the person knowing that the loss of the post could cause great hardship for the family? Such decisions are always difficult and it does not help to gloss over their complexity. Some leaders will always come out on the side of the organization – but in doing so send a clear message to other employees as to their vulnerability if their ability to perform is compromised. The result may be a low level of loyalty to the group. On the other hand, holding on to under-performing staff also sends a poor signal.

In the end a specific decision has to be made. True, it might be a decision with provisos. In the scenario above, the leader may decide to extend the probationary period to ensure that every opportunity is given to the employee to improve. While this might work in some instances, in others, it simply delays the inevitable. Rather than being defensive about the decisions they make, quiet leaders are open about the complexity of some decisions and, provided it doesn't breach matters of confidentiality, are willing to talk about their reasons. In the end they will gently remind others that a definite decision had to be made and that this is the decision that was made. If people have strong opinions about it, the leader will take them into account the next time, though that does not necessarily mean that a different decision will be taken.

Betrayal

There is often a very personal price for leaders to pay. It's why it helps to know why we are doing what we do, and it's important that we are working for something we believe in. Leaders work with people, and people come in all forms. In the Bible we are told that God makes humanity from the dust of the earth and then breathes the dust into life. The image is fascinating. We are both the dust of the earth and the breath of God.[8] At times we see both our own frailty and the frailty of others and it is easy to believe we are from the dust of the earth. This is specially so when others disappoint us or let us down. Quiet leaders are conscious that the trust and confidence that they place in others might be betrayed. They however remain hopeful, remembering that people are also made from the breath of God and might therefore exceed our expectations as they live up to this lofty status. Even while discouraged by those who betray them, they remember that there is another happier side to human personality. They also remember not to take out their disappointment on those who were not responsible for the betrayal. And even when betrayed, they are willing to see what they might learn from the disappointment.

Loneliness

While quiet leaders are collegial and include others in decision-making where possible, in the end they cannot hide behind their team. Just because a decision is unpopular does not make it an incorrect decision. Having to implement unpopular decisions can leave the quiet leader feeling rejected and lonely. Leaders are agents of change, and often the early stages of implementing change can see hostility directed at the leader. Again, a feeling of loneliness is a natural result.

Friendships from outside of one's leadership setting can be enormously helpful during such times, as can the support of one's family. Holding on to the bigger picture of why a particular course of action has been adopted is important.

Weariness

Perhaps you are familiar with Robert Frost's poem, 'Stopping by Woods on a Snowy Evening'.[9] While walking through the forest, Frost notes its beauty. He longs to abandon his journey and to explore the surrounding nooks and crannies, but he knows that if he does so, he will never complete the journey or fulfil the commitments and promises he has made. Reluctantly he reminds himself that he has miles to travel before he can sleep.

The quiet leader knows that they have a task to do. Sometimes the task is ambitious. Often it takes longer than initially thought. Most become quiet leaders because they have found themselves frustrated in groups that are underperforming and know that they can make a difference. At times the road ahead seems long, and they feel weary, but they know that they have promises to keep, and miles to go before they sleep. Because of this, like Myrtle, they keep putting one foot ahead of the next . . . and in due season, they do cross the finish line.

Let's earth this with an interview with a quiet leader . . .

A leadership interview with Nigel Wright

Nigel Wright has been Principal of Spurgeon's College, London, since 2000. A former President of the Baptist Union of Great Britain and the author of over a dozen books, he is listed in *Who's Who* and is widely engaged as a preacher, speaker and lecturer both in the United Kingdom and internationally. I asked him these five questions:

1. Nigel, what do you think? Does the tortoise usually win, and should it?
To answer that with a straightforward Yes or No would betray a host of prejudices. Let's say that a range of leadership styles is needed within the church and we should thank God for those who have great charisma, imagination and style. But that said, the people who are going to see a work through to the point where it can be handed on intact to the next generation are more likely to be of moderate gifting and long-term stickability. I have long been impressed by Nietzsche's 'long obedience in the same direction' and have often prayed that such a grace might be granted to me. It is observable both in history and the present that the great and gifted often have someone working with them who quietly imple-ments their ideas and makes them happen. So, let's hear it for the tortoise! But let's also not forget the need for a mixed economy of leadership styles.

2. Anything you would like to say to those who see themselves as improbable leaders?

The best definition of leadership I have ever come across is that it is to do with 'creating the conditions within which others can thrive'. What I particularly like about this is that it is focused not on the leader but on the others whom the leader is called to serve. It takes up the servant-leader paradigm into itself but at the same time leaves room for flexibility, the ability to bring out of our storehouse things old and new, as needs and conditions require. Anybody who has exercised leadership knows just how much we depend on others working with us to do anything lasting and worthwhile. The 'improbable' leader might take comfort from this because they are under no illusions about their own omnicompetence.

3. Of Allender's five leadership challenges – crisis, complexity, betrayal, loneliness and weariness – which do you struggle with most and why? How do you move beyond it?

I am reasonably acquainted with them all. I have never minded complexity because that's just the way things are. Crisis tends to evoke adrenaline and once weathered successfully can lead to a sense of satisfaction. Loneliness and weariness are commonplace but endurable. So I guess it comes down to betrayal. I would not want to make a big thing of this as though I had experienced much of it. However there have been a few times when people I thought of as friends and supporters have withdrawn their commitment. Sometimes this has been a slow process of alienation caused by changes in health, perspective or spouses. I have felt it most when people have been initiators of new directions then start to criticize the very things they helped to put in motion. There is a balance to be struck between knowing that people can be fickle and taking them on trust. In other words we have to take people at their best but never forget that we are all fallen.

4. Quiet leadership values tenacity and keeping going in spite of the odds. Is there a time to give up, and how do you sense when it has arrived?

There is a time to give up and it is to be perceived in different forms. First of all, there is a time when a job has been done and a burden discharged. 'I have taken them as far as I can' is one of the expressions you hear, and it is legitimate. Personally I have sensed this from time to time and have known the difference (intuitively, I think – I find it hard to say more) between 'There's something I need to see through' and 'It's no longer up to me'. Second, there are times when the energy required to sort out a situation and overcome its complexity is so great that it is better to walk away and devote that energy to something more productive. I don't think we are called to solve every problem, but I do think we are under obligation to end things well to the limit of our abilities. Sometimes this means acknowledging there is a problem you cannot solve but agreeing to disagree with others who are involved or disengaging with good will rather than bitterness.

5. Please pass on one key leadership insight you have.
Only one? I have a list! I happen to believe that although ministry has its complexities it is not rocket-science. Acting and speaking well are at the heart of it. However, human life is replete with opportunities to use the tongue badly and destructively. The book of James is right on this subject. My simple formula (not just for marriage counselling) is, 'There's what he says, there's what she says, and then there's the truth'. We are back to the balance between taking people on trust and being canny in interpreting what they say. I have tried to train myself to be truthful in speech – usually to the point where I understate things in a very British way so as not to exaggerate or inflame. But most people interpret things in a way that serves their own best interests or self-perception and they often seek to cast others in a bad light, as the 'enemy'. Whereas I would not for a moment advocate scepticism or cynicism I think we are wise to think well of people while being careful before we accept their account of things.

For reflection

This is not a book to gallop through. If you read a chapter a day and supplement it with reflection on its relevance to your context, you are likely to get the most from it.

- Spend a moment skimming the chapter again. Do you identify with the tortoise or the hare?
- Which views of leadership most closely reflect your own? Why?
- Were there any gaps between your potential and actual in the four areas of charisma, position, influence and outcomes?
- Are there any actions you should take to bridge the gap?
- Do you identify with any (or all) of the five leadership struggles – crisis, complexity, betrayal, loneliness and weariness?
- Are there some resources that could help you cope with them better?

2

Servant, Shepherd and Steward: A Theology of Quiet Leadership

You know the rulers of the Gentiles lord it over them, and their high officials exercise authority over them. Not so with you. Instead, whoever wants to be great among you must be your servant, and whoever wants to be first must be your slave – just as the Son of Man did not come to be served, but to serve, and to give his life as a ransom for many – Matthew 20:25–8

You've probably met some leaders who personify the stereotype of the toxic leader. Somewhat tyrannical and egotistical, their organization (and it is *their* organization) runs around their whims and idiosyncrasies. It's their way or the highway, and internal dissent is quickly squashed by getting rid of whoever was foolish enough to question the status quo. While these leaders inevitably have some strengths (no one would have started to follow them otherwise) it is fairly obvious that the organization wouldn't stand up to close scrutiny. The group works hard at its public image, usually focusing on appearances rather than reality, and those who are satisfied with what's happening are happy because they have been foolish enough to believe their own publicity.

By contrast we have usually benefited from leaders who work quietly and conscientiously to ensure that their organization flourishes and grows. They include others in their decision-making, but aren't swayed by every voice. They know where they are going and won't be sidetracked. They affirm and recognize others, especially noticing the contribution that each makes and helping ensure that it is both acknowledged and optimized. When the going is tough, they see things through. They always knew they had signed up for the long term, and that even the best years have a range of seasons. They are quiet leaders, and those who follow their lead feel a sense of security in knowing that they are there.

This second style of leadership is far more closely aligned to the best examples of leadership we find in the Bible. The Bible is both descriptive and prescriptive. Some of its descriptive accounts explore unfortunate examples of leadership. Most of the kings of Israel fall into this category. Even King David, a better role model than most, was an adulterer, murderer and a poor father – not insignificant flaws! Other leadership examples are more heartening, such as Joseph and Daniel, and they allow us to extract prescriptive principles from their lives. Not that we should overlook the flawed examples of leadership as they teach us what we should avoid. Naturally enough, as in life, most of the Bible's leaders were strong in some areas, disappointing in others. There is much we can model from Moses; there is equally much we should avoid.

The term 'servant leadership' is often attached to biblical models of leadership.[1] The paradoxical linking of these two words is one of the key features of most of the writing on leadership that flows from Christian authors. For example, Robert Greenleaf in his book *Servant Leadership* argues that leadership is 'bestowed' upon a person who is 'by nature a servant'. The first thing to look for is the servant nature of a person, as this cannot be taken away. It represents the real person (one who desires to serve). Leadership then becomes the way in which the person serves – and it is given if this is something the person is able to do well.[2] If the person is not able to serve via leadership, they will still serve the group, though they will find other ways in which to do so. Indeed, most often a person is appointed to leadership after helpfully serving in a number of other capacities first. It is probably this sequence that Paul has in mind when he instructs Timothy to 'Never be in a hurry about appointing an elder'.[3] We should first see what abilities a person has, and also be confident that giftedness is backed by an appropriate disposition and lifestyle.

The Bible is very affirming about the value of leadership and is clear that the desire to serve via the gift of one's leadership is honourable. 1 Timothy 3:1 (NEB) says simply, 'To aspire to leadership is an honourable ambition.' It is honourable because it is about the desire to serve others, and to help others and their groups become more than they otherwise would be.

Well – that's the theory at any rate! In reality, there is often a shadow side to the quest to lead.

Those who lead hold power as leadership is about influence and being able to play a significant role in determining direction, staff appointments, the use of finance, and so on. The abuse of power can be a subtle temptation. In addition, leaders are sometimes considered to be a little larger than life. The praise and flattery of followers can lead to arrogance, pride and self-righteousness. Some people become leaders because they feel unsuccessful unless they lead. They can become addicted to the adrenaline rush that accompanies being able to set direction, and the admiration that follows those who lead effectively. The journey of leading for the good of the group to leading for the sake of one's own ego can be short, and is sometimes embarked upon subtly. Some leaders are driven to lead, and feel incomplete if they do not have others in tow, and will sometimes act irresponsibly to ensure that this situation remains.

Quiet leaders are usually a different breed. They often come to their task a little reluctantly. They are conscious of the responsibility of helping to set the direction for a group of people or for an organization. They are willing to set aside their leadership if the interests of the group would be better served by another – especially if it is clear that this would be true over the longer term, and not just for a specific project or task. We'll explore this in a little more detail as we ask what servant leadership is and why it is a biblical ideal.

So what is servant leadership and why is it a biblical ideal?

In Christian thought, servant leadership works in two clear directions, as well as in a third, less obvious one.

On the one hand we are servants of Christ who has called us. In his letter to the Philippians, Paul describes Timothy and himself as servants of Jesus Christ; the actual Greek term used denoting a servant who has voluntarily chosen to remain and serve his owner, even when going free was an option.[4] Quiet leaders who identify themselves with the cause of Christ see themselves as called to serve Jesus. They remember that they are not ultimately in charge, and are aware that the lead they give should be in response to the lead they receive from Christ. In short, they feel confident to lead only because they are led. True, the best quiet leaders are not dogmatic about the lead they have been given, and are willing to test the guidance they believe they have received from God with others. Indeed, what often starts as a tentative feeling that God might be nudging in a particular direction is usually confirmed or diluted by discussion with other Christians.

If Christian leaders are first servants of Christ, they are secondly called to serve those who follow their lead. It's at this point that we need to clarify what we mean by servant leadership. In Ephesians 5:21 Paul instructs Christians to 'submit to one another out of reverence for Christ'. The willingness to put the needs of others ahead of one's own is therefore commanded of all Christians. The way we best do this is by asking how we can most effectively serve the needs of the other – how we can be a servant to them. Servant leaders are able to attach the title *leader* to their servanthood because the best way they serve the needs of others is through the leadership they offer.

Contrary to some images that portray servant leaders as rushing around to meet the every whim of those they serve, servant leaders have made the hard-headed decision as to the best way they can serve others. Deserting their leadership role to fulfil tasks that a hundred other people can perform is to abandon their duty – it serves the interests of no one. Quiet leaders quickly figure this out. They know where they are best used. Again, contrary to popular thought, this often comes at a fair personal sacrifice. Actually it's often a lot easier to wash the dishes or put away the chairs after an event than it is to sit down and carefully evaluate what worked well, what didn't and what we might need to do differently next time. There are usually enough people who are capable of vacuuming the carpet, but relatively few who can constructively and realistically review an event and assess where it places us and what actions might now be required from us. Quiet leaders recognize that they have to make sure that the careful work of reflection gets done. True, from time to time they might feel it is appropriate to help with the dishes as well – so long as they don't use it as an excuse to keep them from doing the work they are really called to serve the group by performing. A leaderless group with sparkling carpets and clean dishes is to be pitied, not envied – it will go nowhere even if it has spotless china to accompany it!

So quiet servant leaders follow the lead of Christ and serve the best interests of the group they are called to lead. There is however one other dimension that should be explored.

The Christian church was birthed by God's willingness to send his son Jesus to come and to live among us. The model is one of incarnation – of being there. It's also a model of searching for those who were not already following God. Jesus annoyed the religious leaders of his day by his insistence that he had come to seek and to save the lost. That often meant he worked outside of the tidy zone of what was considered acceptable for the religious people of his day. He regularly reinterpreted the rules of the religious authorities to ensure they served the interests of those who were on the outside.

An example of this is in his paradigm-transforming approach to the Sabbath day, and the laws that had been built around observing the Sabbath. Jesus' observation that the Sabbath was made for people and not people for the Sabbath inverted the way in which the question was approached.[5] Rather than ask what we must do to keep the Sabbath, he insists the focus shift to ensure that Sabbath rules enhance human existence, because that's why the idea of a Sabbath exists. Put differently, Jesus is insisting that the focus be on how the public are best served, not how the organizational stakeholders are best served. Truth to tell, the Sabbath laws as devised by the Pharisees were very convenient for the Jewish leadership – but Jesus refused to allow their interests to dominate.

This principle is important and is one that Christian quiet leaders need to ponder. At times we lead groups where narrow self-interest is the dominant driver for the group. By way of example, some churches organize their programmes in such a way that they are of little use to the broader community, even though they are helpful for what is often a very small church congregation. Christian quiet leaders are conscious of a third source of accountability

– the wider group who should benefit from what the group offers, but who perhaps are not involved at present because of the way in which things are structured. They are willing to advocate for those who are not yet included because their vision is larger – they see both what the group currently is, and what it could be if its vision was more expansive.

It is interesting that when God calls Abram (later to become Abraham) he informs Abram that through him all the nations of the world will be blessed.[6] All too quickly the Hebrew people forgot that the reason for their election to the special status of God's own people was that all would be blessed through them. The purpose of their being blessed was to enable them to have something to offer to others. Sadly, instead of holding to this outward focus required by the call of Abram, they quickly became inwardly tilted. By inward-tilting I mean the tendency to evaluate any action by whether it is for our personal or immediate group good as opposed to an outward-tilting, which assesses the worth of an activity by the value it adds to those who are not yet part of our group.

To summarize then, Christian leadership recognizes three realms of accountability. First the Christian leader is accountable to God, second to the people they are called to lead and third to the group of people who should benefit by what the group is doing but who are currently outside of its orbit. While we could suggest a fourth realm of accountability, namely that the leader is accountable to their own self, perhaps that obscures the fact that servant leadership is on behalf of others and not about the leader's own needs.

Let's make this tangible with an example. The principal of a Christian school is first accountable to God, is second accountable to the board, staff, parents and pupils of the school and, third, is also answerable to the wider community who should benefit by the presence of the school – but who may not benefit at present because of policies or practices that make it difficult to become a part of the school. Because this third group has no legal claim on the school and might say nothing of its irrelevance to them, they are often forgotten when we review the effectiveness of the leadership that is being provided.

One further point about servant leadership. At times servant leaders are called to make difficult decisions, decisions that may be painful and that might isolate the leader. Mary Evans explores the relevance of the servant song found in Isaiah 53 for leaders, noting that as it speaks prophetically about Jesus, those who follow his model of leadership are likely to face similar struggles. She writes:

> It is not a very appealing prospect for God's servant leaders to see part of their role as being despised and rejected, familiar with pain, and giving up all glory for the benefit of those whose sorrows we may be called to carry. But does not the example and teaching of Jesus mean that this is indeed part of our calling to follow him?[7]

Those who embark upon leadership for the benefit of their own ego inevitably abandon ship at this point. Only quiet leaders who embark upon leadership from a sense of call – albeit often a call reluctantly answered – are willing to keep going when the cost becomes personal. They keep putting one foot in front of the other because, like Myrtle in our opening parable, they know that this is the only way to reach the finish line, and they are committed to getting there.

Follower-focused leadership

John Sweetman, principal of Malyon College in Brisbane, Australia, makes the fascinating observation that Christian leadership is follower-focused.[8] He develops a theology of Christian leadership from a follower's perspective, suggesting that Christian leaders begin by asking what God calls them to provide for those he asks them to lead. It's an important insight, and one that I'd like to develop further.

Sweetman outlines six ways in which leaders make provision for those who follow their lead:

1. Christian leaders provide God's *presence* through honouring and needing God
2. Christian leaders provide *security* (through the growth of godly character)
3. Christian leaders provide *significance* (through a servant-heart for people)
4. Christian leaders provide *hope* (through God-given vision)

5. Christian leaders provide *growth* (through equipping followers)
6. Christian leaders provide *empowerment* (through team effectiveness).[9]

Think through each of these headings. What might they mean in your setting? While I won't develop each of these themes, perhaps you will be able to sense the approach (and thus deduce the likely line of argument), by noting some reasons for point 2 – Christian leaders provide security.

Sweetman highlights that security is provided for followers by consistency. It is very unsettling to have a leader who is enthusiastic about something one day, and then indifferent (or even hostile) towards it the next. It leaves followers uncertain how to proceed. A godly character has contours that form in a consistent manner. They include:

- Spiritual growth (Phil. 3:12; 1 Tim. 3:6; 1 Tim. 6:11)
- Integrity (1 Tim. 3:2)
- Purity (1 Tim. 4:12)
- Knowing God and the Bible (Titus 1:9)
- Wisdom (Eph. 5:15–17; Prov. 1:1–7; Jas 3:17)
- Gentleness (1 Tim. 3:3; 6:11; 2 Tim. 2:24–5; Titus 1:7)
- Good reputation, consistency (1 Tim. 3:7)
- Faithfulness (Gal. 5:22)
- Commitment (1 Cor. 9:24–7)
- Humility (1 Tim. 3:6; 1 Pet. 5:5–6)
- Repentance (1 John 1:9–10)
- Submission to authority (Heb. 13:7; 1 Thess. 5:12–13; 1 Pet. 2:13)
- Right motives (1 Tim. 3:3; 1 Pet 5:1–3)
- Contentment (1 Tim. 6:6)
- Generosity (1 Tim. 6:18)
- A teachable spirit (Heb. 13:7)
- Self-discipline (1 Tim. 3:2; Titus 1:8; 1 Pet. 5:8)
- Coping with hardship (2 Tim. 2:3)
- Endurance (1 Tim. 6:11)
- Godly example (Phil. 3:17; 1 Tim. 4:12; 1 Pet. 5:3)

If you struggle to see why these qualities give security to followers, imagine trying to follow someone who has the opposite qualities

– for example, someone who is foolish, rather than wise, or arrogant rather than humble, or who gives up readily rather than seeing things through in tough periods. Take some moments for self-reflection. If those who follow your lead were to rate you on each of these qualities, which would be the ones they would score you highly on, and which would be at the lower end of the scale? Of course you don't need to speculate! You can simply ask some who follow your lead to rate you from 1 to 10, and think through the results afterwards.

Perhaps you are not leading and wonder why others are reluctant to follow the lead you would like to give. Could it be that they sense that some of these qualities are missing in you? A key feature of quiet leadership is that it tries to take the mystery out of leading. Rather than put things into a too hard basket, be willing to ask if there are some areas you might need to change in. This list provides a helpful place to begin.

A key question to ask in evaluating leaders and their leadership (be it our own, or someone else's) is what happens to those who follow their lead. Are their abilities enhanced? Are they more likely to reach their dreams? Do their families fare well? Is their time and energy used constructively? These are probing questions. Some leaders are so task-oriented that they forget to ask what is likely to happen to those who help them to accomplish the task they attempt to achieve. Some worthy projects are marred by the unacceptable price tag paid by those who worked to make the project possible. Servant leaders do not avoid asking these hard questions as they know they have to answer for what becomes of the lives of those who are willing to follow their lead.

Some other biblical images of leadership

Our focus has been on the image of servant leadership. While this is a key biblical image, there are others.

Shepherd

An important leadership image in Scripture is that of shepherd. The shepherd is there for the sake of the sheep. It can be a daunting role. As Derek Tidball writes: 'The Bible seems to make no effort to avoid the small print in its job description of the shepherd. To be a shepherd is costly; to be a good shepherd may well cost one one's life. As the good shepherd, Jesus knew that he was required to lay down his life for his sheep (John 10:11).'[10]

At times a good shepherd has to actively defend the sheep. Confrontation may be required – think of King David's struggles to protect his sheep in his shepherding days, where on occasion he had to rescue his flock from bears and lions.[11] While such literal predators are not as common today, metaphorical ones frequently arise. It takes valour to confront them. Quiet leaders know that they have to go in and bat for their staff. At times they have to be very vocal about what constitutes an acceptable workload, fair pay or reasonable responsibilities.

Sometimes the shepherd has to protect the flock from its own tendency to self-destruct. The shepherd guides to places which are safe and nurturing. Contemporary parallels for quiet leaders might be steering employees away from gossip and in-house bickering, or from endlessly focusing on problems rather than working towards solutions. Many people have grown up in an environment of criticism and negativity. They quickly reproduce this in the workplace unless they are guided towards life-affirming models that help them to note the positives. Quiet leaders shepherd people by modelling ways to spot signs of hope in each situation. Hope energizes people, while discouragement flattens most. Quiet leaders steadily work at boosting morale and hopefulness.

A key responsibility of the shepherd is to ensure the sheep are well fed. While the importance of this to someone who is the pastor of a church is obvious, don't miss its importance for those who are in other positions of leadership. Ensuring one's sheep are well fed may mean looking out for professional development opportunities for one staff member while flicking on details of a helpful internet site to another, and taking time to debrief on performance with yet another. The basic concern is simple. Quiet leaders know that there are not only tasks to be completed, but people to be nurtured and developed along the way. This is implicit in the image of the leader as shepherd. Naturally efforts to stretch and develop staff may be looked at with suspicion by some who could view them as a vote of no confidence unless the leader has built a solid relationship with the staff team. Jesus teaches that the shepherd is able to direct the flock because the sheep follow the voice they know and trust.[12]

There are many ways in which this can be achieved. Sometimes it is about remembering to walk through the workplace slowly. Wise quiet leaders don't rush to their office as quickly as possible. They linger in the corridors, asking about the welfare of staff, taking an interest in what others are engaged in, intentionally noting and commenting on what is going well, rather than trying to spot errors. All this helps build morale, and ensures that the leader remains in touch with what others are thinking, feeling and doing.

It is easy to test if we are shepherding the people in our orbit. What do we hope they will become? What do they hope to become? What doors do we hope will open for them? What doors do they hope will open for them? Are we doing anything to increase the likelihood of their dreams coming true? If not, we're probably passive rather than active shepherds.

Steward

If servant leadership refers to a disposition that is willing to serve via leadership, and shepherding to the attitude we have towards those we serve, stewardship is the primary practice of the Christian leader. The leader is to have an attitude of accountability.[13] Although Christian leaders often struggle with resources that seem inadequate, they don't forget that they have often been provided by the generosity of others, sometimes at fair personal cost. They are also conscious that ultimately all resources come from God. They are therefore anxious to ensure that they are used effectively.

Luke 12:42–6 makes it clear that a steward is a servant who is wholly and unconditionally accountable to their master. While a steward is a leader, none of their ruling authority is for their own benefit. There is therefore nothing intrinsically selfish about being a good steward. It is not about wringing the last cent out of an investment to secure a yet more luxurious retirement home. It is about overseeing God's resources for the good of God's work in the world.

It does of course mean that leaders think long and hard about whom they are serving and what cause they are working for. If an effective leader works for an essentially evil cause (or less dramatically, an indifferent cause), they might be an effective steward for evil, or simply be a good steward for something trivial. In the bigger picture, while they might have been a successful steward of their company's resource, they might not have been a good steward of their own time and gifting. In short, quiet leaders sometimes come to the conclusion that they are wasting their time where they are and that their abilities would be better utilized elsewhere. Naturally such a decision is never made lightly, but part of good stewardship involves a willingness to raise these kinds of troubling questions.

There are some key biblical principles to being a good steward. Think of a few which are found in Matthew 25:14–30, a story that Jesus told which is often called 'The Parable of the Talents'. It's the story where a man going on a journey asks three of his servants to look after a different quantity of his goods while he is away. One is given five bags of gold, another, two and another one. During the absence of the owner, the first two double his assets, while the third, a more timid individual, buries the single bag of gold entrusted to him, thereby not losing the asset but, equally, not adding to it. Needless to say, on his return the owner is delighted with the first two, and unimpressed with the third. He allows the first two to remain as stewards of the larger asset base they now have, and indeed expands the holding of the first even further by giving them the single bag of gold originally allocated to the one who did nothing. In the end, the first servant has to steward eleven bags of gold, the second four, while the third has none.

Principles flow thick and fast from this parable. Think of a few ...

Where we start is not where we end. None of the three finishes in the same position that they started in. There is therefore little point in bemoaning our starting point, because it is fluid and will change as time goes by.

Or there is the principle that those who prove faithful in little things will be faithful with larger things. We know this one is valid. When we have a vacancy at work we most commonly look at those a rung below and ask who is doing a good job and is ready for additional responsibility, and promote accordingly. It would be very strange to decide to appoint someone who was underperforming in their current post.

And there are others . . . Those who are faithful with what belongs to others can be trusted with goods of their own. Those who use their gifts can be entrusted with more. Those who bury their gifts lose them – and so we could go on. Don't forget that as Jesus is the storyteller, it is probably not too much of a stretch to suggest that there is even an implication that those who can handle material things can be entrusted with spiritual goods.

Responsible stewardship operates in many areas and is not limited to the realm of finance. It can be of the truths of Scripture, or of the buildings owned by a Christian community, or of the reputation a Christian school has in an area or of the range of gifts represented in the people we lead. Luther Snow has written an informative book entitled *The Power of Asset Mapping* in which he explores the importance of tracking the full range of assets present within any group of people or organization.[14] Following the work of McKnight and Kretzmann, he suggests we think in terms of five asset types:

1. Physical assets: These are things we can touch and see. It might be land, equipment or the natural beauty of our environment.
2. Individual assets: These include the talents, skills and overall experience of the individuals in our organization, or whom we are able to draw upon.
3. Associational assets: Here we include the networks and voluntary groups which we are part of. They might be more formal professional groups or less formal groups of like-minded volunteers.
4. Institutions: Here we look at other agencies with budget and staff with whom we have contact. For a local church, it could be their denominational headquarters and the assistance they can provide; for a school, the state educational authorities.
5. Economic assets: These involve money, and include our spending power, investments, and our ability to produce goods and services for which people are willing to pay.[15]

Carefully mapping the resources we have in each of these areas is usually liberating, most groups discovering that they have larger assets than they realized. It also helps define the scope of our stewardship, as we explore how effectively we utilize the full range of our contacts and possessions.

Another key area of stewardship is in the use of time – both in the way we use our own time, as well as if we make it possible for those we lead to steward their time wisely. A badly run meeting that starts late and meanders in no particular direction represents poor stewardship not only of the leader's time, but of every group member who has to be present. If there are eight people present and the meeting drags on for two hours, two working days have been wasted. Often giving an extra hour to prepare for the meeting could have made all the difference. Likewise a sermon delivered to two hundred people that lasts for thirty minutes but has been poorly planned and says nothing of any significance, has effectively wasted one hundred hours of time – that's two and a half working weeks. An extra two hours of preparation time might have redeemed those one hundred hours and could have helped ensure that something of value occurred during that time. All of these are important stewardship questions, and quiet leaders take them seriously.

At times good stewardship involves saying no to some things. A staff member might enjoy giving us a blow-by-blow account of their every activity, but listening might represent a poor stewardship of our time – and of theirs. Sometimes we fool ourselves into believing that we are simply being nice (or polite) to others, when we are actually allowing time for both of us to be wasted. Leaders who are good stewards find ways to slip out of such scenarios without being offensive or indifferent to the talkative and lonely. The best leaders help others to become involved in a story that is worth talking about . . . They often help people to abandon a story that is going nowhere, and invite them to participate in building a legacy that can be spoken of with pride. If at times that means that we have to help people to shift their focus, so be it. It is a small price to pay.

When images collide

Leaders deal with complexity. Emphasizing one image of leadership might see the leader abandoning another. Take the implicit tension between being a shepherd and a steward. At times it can be difficult to shepherd someone and to hold them to account for the poor use of the organization's time or resources. Many leaders abandon the shepherding role because they find it too difficult to juggle chaplaincy-type responsibilities while also holding people accountable. At times people underperform. One can't say 'great work' when the task has been done indifferently. While the dilemma is understandable, it helps to differentiate between short- and long-term outcomes. A sympathetic pastoral conversation that avoids asking hard questions might be pleasant in the short term, but in the longer term might do the person a serious disservice in that it might help to reinforce unhelpful patterns of behaviour. While leaders cannot be all things to all people (and should avoid the risk of trying to be), in the longer term there is not really a contradiction between the need to shepherd followers and to act as a diligent steward by requiring accountability.

Beyond the three s's

If you are limited to three biblical metaphors of leadership, you can't do better than the three s words – servant, shepherd and steward. Fortunately, no such limit need apply. There are other rich biblical images relevant for leadership. In his book *Builders and Fools*, Derek Tidball explores the leader as ambassador, athlete, builder, fool, parent, pilot, scum and shepherd.[16] Each is richly suggestive. I'd add that leaders are dreamers, poets, heralds of hope. They are gentle optimists, realistically facing problems but refusing to allow them the last word. Perhaps you have some images of your own.

A leadership interview with Derek Tidball

Derek Tidball was formerly the Principal of the London School of Theology, and is the author of numerous books, including an influential book on leadership, *Builders and Fools*.

1. This chapter has explored three key images of leadership, those of servant, shepherd and steward. In your book on leadership, Builders and Fools, *you explore a number of others. If you were forced to chose one image of leadership as being the most important, which would it be, and why?*
The one image I would choose for pastoral leadership is curiously one that occurs only once in passing, that of the pilot or navigator.

The word *kybernetēs* occurs in 1 Corinthians 12:28 and in older translations was often translated poorly as 'administrator'. It's a dynamic and evocative image, much taken up by the early church, which focuses on the skill of moving a ship and its crew through changing conditions and obstacles to a destination. Our destination is the day when the church will be presented to Christ.

2. Some images of leadership are a little paradoxical. The shepherding leader also has to be a good steward. Sometimes the two feel incompatible. Please give your insight into ways to move beyond the possible impasse.
I agree. 'Servant leadership' can be especially difficult. There are two ways to reconcile them. First, reality is much more complex than simple concepts allow. So, being a parent is simultaneously a position of authority and of service. Parents take decisions, but also serve as cleaners, taxi drivers and everything else their children need! Second, some images are paradoxical because God's style is profoundly counter-cultural. He leads and accomplishes his will not by domineering but by serving. Our problem with the images arises because we are too governed by a secular mindset of leadership.

3. Name a leader you resonate with in the Bible, and unpack why.
I am particularly fond of Barnabas. He exemplifies leadership not as the 'A-type', extrovert type of leader but leadership as quiet influence. He encouraged the 'unauthorized' church in Antioch because 'he saw what the grace of God had done'. He kept a clear focus rather than being concerned about trivial niceties. He courageously sought out the recently-converted Paul and invested in him and stood by young Mark when he couldn't keep up the pace. His influence was immense in building a church, mentoring an apostle and preparing a young man for life-long service. Deep investment in people is what excites me about leadership. And we know he was a man of integrity and this wasn't a professional act because he sold his property for the cause of the gospel.

4. If you were starting out on your leadership journey today, what would you do differently?
Many, many things. I would seek a mentor, a concept which is fairly common today but was just not there when I began in ministry forty years ago. Looking back, I think I might have paced

myself differently. I've been in the fast lane for most of those years and it has taken its toll. But I'm praying for faithfulness, vitality and what Gordon MacDonald calls 'resilience' right to the last. Then, pursuing the image of the pilot, there are times when I would have handled the tiller differently. Most leadership is not about grand plans and great visions but day-to-day decisions; hence having the hand on the tiller is an appropriate metaphor. It's vital to know when to push an issue and stand firm and when to let matters go as unimportant. Most of us have the temptation to be overly dogmatic about non-essentials rather than following in the footsteps of Barnabas and keeping our eye on 'the grace of God' at work.

5. Please pass on one key leadership insight you have.
Leadership demands people-skills. We may have theology at our fingertips, graduated with MBAs, exercised great charismatic gifts, and attended the latest conferences, but unless we love people we'll fail. We'll fail on pragmatic grounds. People are more committed and best motivated when they are loved, rather than used or driven. We also fail on spiritual grounds; 1 Corinthians 13 makes that clear. Our calling is to follow Jesus and adopt his leadership-style. He 'loved the church and gave himself up for her' (Eph. 5:25). Many failures in leadership occur because of inept handling or failure to love people.

For reflection

Think about the three images of Christian leadership we have explored: servant, shepherd and steward.

- What implication does each image have for your setting?
- Are there any ways in which your current practice might change if you were to allow yourself to be shaped by these images?
- In what ways are you a servant in your leadership?
- And a shepherd?
- And a steward?

3

Becoming and Doing: Ethics and Virtues which Shape Quiet Leaders

All leaders have to make decisions. Even a refusal to decide is, in itself, a decision. One of the great differences between leaders and followers is that while followers have the luxury of critiquing decisions, leaders have to make them. The outcome of our leadership is closely linked to the calibre of the decisions we make – did we decide for or against purchasing a property, for or against employing an extra staff member, for or against launching a new product . . . and so it goes on. It is important to consider how we go about making decisions.

Pragmatic leaders decide on the basis of what they think is most likely to succeed at the time – and clearly this is a dimension of decision-making that cannot be ignored. It is hard to motivate a group of people to do something that you think is unlikely to succeed.

More reflective leaders are aware that there are a range of factors to be taken into account before a verdict is reached. They often agonize over the realization that many decisions have winners and losers. While it's nice to aim for win–win solutions, finding them can prove elusive.

Most decisions have ethical implications. We'll explore the three most common approaches adopted when making moral choices – those advocated by deontological ethicists, teleological ethicists and virtue ethicists. If this is unfamiliar territory for you, don't be deterred by the names! You've probably used each of the approaches, even if unaware that it represented a school of thought. Often people unconsciously mix and match the approaches. Singling them out will help make us aware of the factors we give weight to when we make choices. It can also help us to understand why some reach different decisions from our own. We might even make different decisions in future, once we are a little more aware of what is at stake in each stance.

In addition, leadership itself is an ethical challenge. Most leaders face many temptations. It is a rare leader who never contemplates abusing the power inherent in leadership. The mystique that some-times surrounds leaders can see them exposed to sexual temptations that others might avoid. The potential to abuse funds is always a risk . . . and the list could continue to expand. Suffice to say that quiet leaders should equip themselves with sufficient ethical insight to steer them through the moral minefield they are likely to face.

Deontological ethics

Those who embrace deontological ethics look for clear rules to guide them. One rule might be that people should always tell the truth. If we adopt this rule, but deliberately distort or conceal aspects of a project to ensure that it will be approved, we have fallen short of the ethical standard we have set. For example, if a building company is keen for a project to be approved and speaks about the economic benefits of the project while doing all in its power to conceal aspects of a study that reported negatively on its likely environmental impact, most would agree that the company has been less than honest. A very basic element of deontological ethics has been violated in that the company has been selective in what it has reported and has withheld important items of infor-mation to increase the likelihood of a go-ahead being given.

In this example the failure to tell the truth is passive as the company simply chose to say nothing about the negative report. They didn't claim the report was positive. If they had, that would have been active deceit. While active deceit is easy to spot, moral leaders often have to grapple with issues related to passive deceit, which can be far more subtle and therefore more easily ignored. Passive deceit often operates at the level of creating an impression without explicitly making direct claims.

There are many other rules which might guide us. Most accept that we should not steal, and that we should not kill and that we should not be unkind to others. Loosely speaking when we look for rules to guide us in our decision-making we are embracing a moral framework known as deontological ethics. A key task in this approach is to decide which rules we will adopt. Many Christians and Jews adopt the Ten Commandments for their deontological framework.[1] Naturally when we adopt such a frame we need to know what we mean by each of our rules. For example, what do we mean by stealing (does it include underpaying workers?), or killing (does it include causing the death of the enemy in war?) and what does being kind or unkind mean (is it kindness for the greatest number if you can't figure out a way to be kind to all?)?

Teleological ethics

A second ethical framework focuses on the likely outcome of actions we might take. Sometimes known as consequentialist ethics, it is also related to what can be called teleological ethics, where the focus is on the goal one wishes to attain. Leaders sometimes face an ethical dilemma when the rules they have adopted reduce the likelihood of their attaining the goal they are striving for. An all too common example is when workers have to be retrenched to ensure that a company meets its financial target. At this point the deontological principle to act with kindness conflicts with the goal of meeting financial markers. We should not trivialize the latter. If a company consistently fails to make an adequate profit, it will soon not be able to employ any workers. Some of the most painful and difficult leadership decisions are made at such times.

It is helpful to recognize that the dilemma flows from having conflicting moral obligations. Conflicting moral obligations are one of the most common reason we face ethical dilemmas. We want to go the extra mile for our company, and also to be an excellent parent – sadly the day doesn't expand to twenty-seven hours to accommodate the conflict. Working out a hierarchy of priorities can help at such times. It can also ensure that the obligation not met is neither glossed over nor trivialized. Those who adopt a teleological approach look to the longer term rather than the immediate. They decide on the basis of what is likely to ensure that the overall goals are met, even if that requires violating some other-wise sound deontological rules. Thus, for example, telling a lie might be acceptable if it ensures that a worthy project goes ahead. The long-term good is seen to outweigh the current compromise.

Virtue ethics

A third approach to ethics is to focus on virtues which we should cultivate. In virtue ethics, the focus is on neither rules nor conse-quences of behaviour, but on the character of the moral agent. While virtuous people might embark upon misguided activi-ties, acting in accord with virtue will usually result in virtuous outcomes. This approach is often adopted by people who fear that a deontological approach to ethics will make one too inflexible, while a consequentialist approach is too unpredictable – can we ever really know the outcome of our decisions in advance? This is especially true when we ponder how many decisions have unin-tended outcomes. Parents agreeing to their daughter's request for a toy might be laying down a foundation for a selfish and spoilt attitude in her later life but, equally, turning down the request could contribute to a growing despair in the girl so that she comes to believe that she will never be able to get what she really wants. The bottom line is that we can never be sure of the outcome (or outcomes) of a decision. In the light of this, virtue ethicists advo-cate that we embrace certain virtues. The virtues to be adopted vary according to the virtue ethicist followed, but common choices include generosity, patience and kindness.

In virtue ethics one does not act in a virtuous manner because a rule dictates that one should do so. Thus while a deontologist who adopts truth-telling as a rule will tell the truth because of the rule, a virtue ethicist who adopts honesty as a virtue will tell the truth because they are truthful – the virtue is part of who they are.

While some would argue that values and virtues are synony-mous, it is probably better to make a slight distinction between them. Values are something that you have and that are based upon your particular social, cultural, or political circumstances. They are therefore more related to time and context. Virtues, on the other hand, are more abstract principles that can adjust to changing circumstances. While a virtue might express itself in a different way in different eras, the essential virtue does not change over time.

A case-study

Life is not always tidy, and quiet leaders discover this all too quickly. At times leaders may not be able to act in accordance with the virtues that most naturally flow from them. They might be generous, but compelled to act in a frugal manner to ensure the long-term survival of the company. They might be honest, but feel obligated to be less than transparent because they realize their transparency might be manipulated and used to the detriment of others.

Most commonly adopted rules, likely consequences and embraced virtues are in dynamic interaction with each other. As Lovin puts it: 'Neither goals nor rules alone provide enough guidance for our choices to show us how to live a good life. But a good life seen as a whole seems to require something more even than goals and rules together. To have a good life we need goals to achieve and rules to follow, but we also need to understand who we are as persons.'[2] This holistic understanding of the wide range of ethical responsibility has much to commend it. When all three realms agree, no ethical dilemma exists. But this is not always the case.

An extended case-study might help. We'll look at an ancient ethical dilemma – dating back around 3,500 years. It's the biblical account of the Hebrew midwives who are placed in the untenable position of being instructed to kill all Hebrew male babies at birth. The account is found in Exodus 1.[3]

Let's then quickly recap the relevant events. A Pharaoh who didn't know the Hebrew leader Joseph, or the way in which Joseph had helped ensure the survival of the Egyptians, has come to power in Egypt. Instead of seeing in the Israelites allies and friends, he views them from the lens of threat and danger, and reduces them to slavery and forced labour. In spite of their dire circumstances, the Hebrews continue to multiply, which simply fuels Pharaoh's paranoia of them. He decides that the best course of action is to kill all male Hebrew babies at birth, and instructs the Hebrew midwives Shiphrah and Puah to be the agents of execution. Aghast at this immoral instruction, they fail to implement it, and in due time are called to account for the continuing existence of male Hebrew babies. They fabricate an outrageous lie, suggesting that Hebrew women are not like Egyptian women, and that they give birth so quickly that the services of a midwife are not required.

In what makes a fascinating study of the foolishness that flows from prejudice, Pharaoh is taken in by their deception. We are told that God is pleased with the actions of the midwives and rewards them with children of their own – a lofty reward at any time in history, but especially in the ancient world. Indeed, the reward is greater than this, for by inserting their names into the passage – Shiphrah and Puah lest you forget them – the author is ensuring that their names will be remembered forever. He does not extend the same courtesy to Pharaoh who remains simply as 'Pharaoh who?' Clearly someone of his ilk does not have a name that is worthy of being remembered.

While the passage is undoubtedly complimentary towards the midwives, there are three fairly obvious criticisms that any responsible ethicist must offer.

First, the midwives were liars. Remember what they said. Hebrew women are not like Egyptian women – their babies are born so easily and swiftly. Was this incredible 'porky' that they told the Pharaoh simply a 'little white lie' to get them out of a tricky situation – something that in the larger picture was of very little consequence? One of the fathers of ethics, Immanuel Kant, would disagree. Kant is remembered for his concept of the categorical imperative. Kant argued that the moral rightness of an act lies in our willingness to universalize the rule of action which generated it. Because people are not stepping stones towards another goal, we have to view each step in our moral journey as an end in itself. For example, if we deceive someone on a journey to 'a noble end' (as the midwives did), we forget that each step of the journey is an end in itself. What if everyone deceived everyone else while trying to accomplish some 'noble end'? If we don't like the picture of the world which would result from universalizing the steps we have taken, the principle we are operating from is likely to be flawed.

Baptist theologian Stanley Grenz summarizes the one impera-tive underlying Kant's deontological theory as: 'Always do the act that is motivated by the sincere belief that what you are doing is the right thing to do, right not merely for you but for anybody seeking to act properly in any similar situation'.[4] Put slightly differently, if one is to break a moral imperative, one has to ask what the conse-quences would be if everyone else acted in the same way.

We could argue that the midwives' deceit should not be consid-ered a lie because they were in the middle of a war – a fight for the survival of the Hebrews. We don't accuse a soccer player who acts as though he is about to swerve to the right, but at the last moment veers left, of being morally suspect. Rather we commend him for his skill. In a similar manner, the rules of war are different from the rules of everyday life. One can never be candid with the enemy.

While not without merit – and probably part of the midwives' own rationale for their behaviour, there is a significant flaw in this justification. Surely one of the requirements of a just war (presup-posing any such category can ever really exist) is that it is openly declared. Pharaoh is clearly unaware that he faces an enemy in the midwives and, while we need feel no obligation to give him excessive sympathy, there is a niggling sense that this is a betrayal by some he had identified as friends and allies.

So does lying matter? Truth to tell, we already live in a world where we are uncertain as to the veracity of most statements we hear. The term 'a truthful politician' is commonly considered an oxymoron, while body-language experts train us to look out for deceit by checking to see if the speaker looks away from us, or covers their lips or brushes their nose.[5] It feels a little sad to live in a world where such skills are necessary. Is this the legacy of too quickly approving of the kind of deceit that the midwives engaged in?

The second criticism is, in my view, even more serious. Not only were the Hebrew midwives liars, they reinforced the stereotype of the Hebrews as 'other'. Given the expressive and dramatic nature of Hebrew culture, we can safely assume that they would have told their tale of Hebrew women with great gusto. Pharaoh prob-ably delighted in every moment of it – and is likely to have chor-tled in delight as he heard how quickly Hebrew women gave birth

– so unlike Egyptian women who were delicate and refined and needed the assistance of a midwife. Those at the forefront of social change know how hazardous such stereotyping can be. Before the 'other' can be accepted, they must be seen not as 'other', but as 'one of us'. Indeed, the 'othering of the enemy' allows the perpetrators of violence to justify their actions.

Pharaoh, if he had access to twenty-first-century terminology, could have said to himself, 'I knew it. They are a genetic aberration. They don't even bear children in the same way as Egyptians. Clearly they are not really people, and therefore their lives are of no value.' That this 'othering' should occur so early in Israel's history is perhaps a sobering prelude to the more recent 'othering' at the hands of Hitler's henchmen. Lest one think that 'othering' is of little consequence, reflect for a while on the outcome of the Nazi holocaust and the reasons which were used to justify it. We might quickly gloss over the tale that these midwives told, but it had the potential to be extraordinarily damaging. That they communicated this stereotype to a Pharaoh who devised policy on the basis of his prejudices was potentially reckless.

A third criticism is that they were only partially successful, stereotyping liars. While in the short term their ingenious fabrication spared their lives, and the lives of some Israelite boys, in the bigger picture, it was a failed strategy. As the midwives didn't kill the Hebrew boys at birth, Pharaoh organized for those babies to be drowned instead. For that, no midwives were required. This was not the end of persecution for the Hebrews; it was simply the turning of the page as a new era, possibly worse than the previous one, emerged. True, there was a brief respite and some lives were saved, but it was a false dawn. The night was to get considerably darker.

For all this, we miss the point of this biblical account if we fail to observe God's clear satisfaction with the actions of Shiphrah and Puah. Their names are remembered and they are rewarded with children of their own. There was no greater reward in the ancient world. So what are we to make of the ethical dilemmas inherent in Exodus 1? Noting these insights can be very liberating for quiet leaders who might at times feel a little like the Hebrew midwives – damned if they do and damned if they don't.

First we should note the obvious. Life is messy, but God is kind in the midst of it. Of course it is not enough to simply note this;

we need to practise it in the grace we show towards those who have found themselves in difficult situations and have made 'best we could think of at the time' decisions. Indeed, quiet leaders should be willing not just to show such grace towards others, but sometimes towards their own selves, if they have been in situations which have been far more complex than they were able to manage. This graciousness can ensure long-term survival both for quiet leaders, and for those who follow them.

Second, the ethical quest is often about finding the optimal path in real-life circumstances. Ethics works its way out in the real world – not the classroom. This is not to devalue the classroom, but to acknowledge that it is a different arena from the one in which our ethical or virtuous living finds its outlet. If what is worked out in the classroom finds no place in daily life, the work of the classroom is not complete.

Third, don't miss the hopefulness of this text. In terms of Jewish literature, Exodus 1 is a passage of great humour. The midwives pull a fast one over Pharaoh. Though Pharaoh seems all-powerful, this shows him to be a bumbling buffoon, fooled by his own prejudice. If the Pharaoh can be tricked, there is hope. While they waited for the turning of the tide, they found some moments to chuckle among themselves. Sometimes laugher is all that oppressed communities can hope for. Sometimes it is the only reason they survive. The laughter would have had to last them a long time. It would be more than eighty years before Moses would lead them to freedom. Neither Shiphrah, nor Puah, nor any of their contemporaries would have been alive when that day finally dawned. A brief moment of laughter was all that they had. They needed to savour it deeply. It was a sign of hope to help keep them going. So too, let's not knock those who are unable to help communities find long-term solutions to their problems, but who find ways to soften the problems with which those communities will continue to live for all too many years. As quiet leaders we may not always be able to find long-term solutions, but helping people to get by in the short term is also important.

Fourth, for all the mistakes the midwives make – lying, stereotyping their own people and doing so for minimal success – they show that they remember what matters most: the saving of life. Put bluntly, in the ethical sphere they realized that saving life trumps truth-telling. Given that they couldn't think of a way to do both, they showed a nuanced and valid set of priorities.

In more despairing moments, given the awful plight that was that of the Hebrews at this time, they might have wondered if these lives were worth sparing. I'm reminded of the haunting lines from the William Blake poem, 'Auguries of Innocence':

Every morn and every night,
Some are born to sweet delight.
Some are born to sweet delight.
Some are born to endless night.[6]

The Hebrew babies saved by these women would have spent their entire lives as slaves. Exodus 1 makes it abundantly clear that they were slaves treated with great cruelty. These were people born to endless night. Would it perhaps have been more humane to let them die at birth?

The reality was that the midwives had no way of knowing how long their current nightmare would continue. They lived in the hopefulness that God would ultimately act and create a better future for them and for their children. For that better future to dawn, they knew that each generation needed to survive. Though not in their lifetime, in the end the day of liberation arrived, and a generation of Hebrews had managed to survive to seize it. Shiphrah and Puah can rightly claim some of the credit for the long-term survival of the Hebrew people.

Fifth, don't overlook the fact that the two heroes in this passage are women. In an age in which we debate – often uncharitably – about the role of men and women, this passage reminds us that the call to genuine heroism is gender-neutral. In this passage, it is two daring women who find the courage to do the right thing. Later it is an anxious but no less courageous male, Moses, who more directly challenges the next Pharaoh. The things that matter most, like being made in the image of God,[7] and doing the right thing, have got nothing to do with gender. It is always tragic if we forget this, and quiet leaders remember the many issues of justice that flow from it.

While the risk of choosing a path of action is that there will be unintended and sometimes undesirable consequences, the greater risk is to do nothing. Whatever mistakes Shiphrah and Puah make, they are women of great courage and they stand out as hopeful signs of resistance to evil.

Some of the virtues of quiet leadership

With this broad overview of ethical theory, we are in a position to apply it a little more systematically to quiet leadership. Most who write on quiet leadership operate from the framework of virtue ethics,[8] but keep in mind the insights of deontological and teleological ethicists as you formulate your own ethical structure.

Five virtues in particular have come to be associated with theories of quiet leadership. These are modesty, restraint, tenacity, interdependence and other-centredness. We will focus briefly on each, highlighting their relevance for quiet leadership.

Modesty

Badaracco writes: 'Quiet leaders are not inclined to think they are changing the world – this sounds a little too grand. Their aim is simply to do their bit.'[9] Quiet leaders recognize that a variety of forces beyond their control contribute to the outcome of any activity. Badaracco goes on to quote John F. Kennedy, who when asked how he became a hero during World War II replied, 'I had no choice, they sunk my boat.'[10] As Proverbs 16:9 says, we can make our plans, 'but the LORD determines [our] steps'.

Recognizing that ability, dedication and drive are only a few of the factors that determine what does or does not happen, quiet leaders see their place within the big picture. Everything does not depend upon them, but equally they are conscious that their skills and dedication make a difference. It requires following the Romans 12:3 instruction: 'Do not think of yourself more highly than you ought, but rather think of yourself with sober judgment, in accordance with the measure of faith God has given you.' Sober judgement is not false humility. It is a realistic appraisal of the part we play within the whole. We are neither the giant of our dreams nor the dwarf of our fears. We aren't responsible for most things that happen – but we can shape and influence some outcomes, and therefore quiet leaders accept the responsibility of doing what they can.

Badaracco writes: 'Situations calling for quiet leadership are usually complicated, uncertain and hazardous. To survive and succeed it is critical to be realistic and not exaggerate how much you really understand.'[11] It takes modesty and humility to acknowledge what we don't know or what we only partially grasp. When we recognize our limited knowledge, we listen more carefully and respectfully to others. This puts us in a good position to make sound decisions.

Restraint

Leaders invariably face situations which are challenging and stressful. It is tempting at such times to dump one's emotions onto others, or to villainize them, or to provide feedback that only focuses on the negatives without acknowledging the broader context of positives that so often exists. Often strong reactions reflect our bias or misunderstanding of a situation. Speaking of this Badaracco writes:

> immediate venting of thoughts and feelings usually resembles the Vietnam War tactic of bombing a village in order to save it. Quiet leaders don't want to repress what they feel, but they do want to control and channel it as effectively as possible. They realize that taking a forceful stand on principle can be the easy way out of a problem or can make matters worse, so they restrain themselves. Moving at Internet speed is a bad mistake for people going in the wrong direction.[12]

A little further he perceptively notes: 'In most cases quiet leadership would not be possible without a good deal of patience and self-discipline. Pausing and waiting give people time to learn, examine nuances, drill down into complexities, and nudge events in the right direction. They let people listen to the quiet voices of intuition and conscience that are so easily drowned out by urgent demands and strong feelings.'[13]

Restraint is not about deliberately delaying decisions or activity. It is about ensuring that enough time is secured to be sure that quality decisions are made. During that time, effective quiet leaders research the issues and consult others about them. Restraint flows from recognizing that leadership is a long-term process. It is not about one dramatic event that changes everything. Wise quiet leaders will sometimes commit themselves to being listeners at meetings, and refuse to enter into the conversation to ensure that their focus is on listening accurately and intently.

Quiet leaders remember that few people regret not having made an acidic or derogatory remark, and are very conscious that the reverse is true. Words once spoken are usually retracted only with pain and embarrassment. They therefore take seriously the instruction found in James 1:19: 'Everyone should be quick to listen, slow to speak and slow to become angry.'

Restraint can operate at another level and influence the pace adopted. Badaracco talks of 'Nudging, testing and escalating gradually' often being 'the best and fastest ways to make the world a better place'.[14] While there are times to move ahead quickly, most often we need to move consistently in the same direction. It's the story of why the tortoise beats the hare all over again.

Tenacity

Quiet leaders usually have the virtue of tenacity. Their tenacity commonly results from their caring deeply about some issues. These issues reflect their values, and also their areas of hopefulness. They sense that if they stick with some things they will be able to make a difference and realize that this is not true of many areas of life. The tenacity of leaders is not arbitrary. If it were, it would simply mean that they were stubborn or inflexible. It flows from a settled belief that certain things matter and that it is possible to make a difference in some areas – even if it is difficult and even though it may take time. At times the conviction is so strong that although there is little likelihood of a successful outcome the leader might stick at it convinced that, regardless of outcome, some issues are worth standing up for.

Tenacity matters because change usually comes slowly, after much work, diplomacy, some setbacks, and disappointments, and the outcomes are often not all that was hoped for. Without perseverance, few get beyond the realm of daydreaming. Some back away from leadership because they realize that at some stage it usually involves compromise and conflict. While quiet leaders are wise enough to aim for win–win solutions, they are not so naïve as to believe that this is always the outcome. They need a strong moral compass to guide them through the potential pitfalls, and the tenacity to persevere beyond disappointments.

The best quiet leaders are able to mix tenacity with restraint. Tenacity keeps one going, whereas restraint alerts one to the need to apply the brakes. A car without brakes is hazardous, but a car with brakes but no accelerator will not go anywhere! Tenacity provides the drive to keep going. When coupled with restraint, it equips the quiet leader to discern those moments when it is better to back away.

Interdependence

Systems theory teaches us that nothing occurs in isolation. Movement in one part of a system has an impact on other parts, which in turn has further ramifications. Systems theory notes that things placed together interact so that the system becomes the conglomeration of its various parts. The overall effect is greater than the sum of its parts, with the interrelationships between different parts of the system often creating new reactions.

Culbertson quotes Rosenblatt: 'In systems theory, a person is not a freestanding, constant entity but achieves her or his nature of the moment through interaction. In different relationships the individual is different and is defined by others – and defines himself or herself – differently.'[15]

The question 'Who am I?' cannot therefore really be answered. I am in relationship to others. As those relationships change, I change. Not that I am simply my relationships, but I can never understand myself outside of them. Certainly the Bible stresses the importance of standing in relationship with others, with the first 'not good' in the Bible given to the aloneness of Adam before the creation of Eve.[16] In Pauline thought, it is 'together with all the saints' (and perhaps only together with them) that we are able to begin to understand the height, depth and breadth of Christ's love.[17]

Quiet leaders recognize the inevitability of interdependence and value it. It is part of the reason for their modesty. It does not all depend upon them. They are always strongly dependent upon the input and performance of others. They are also liberated by it. We do make a difference in the lives of others. Our interrelatedness means that we can intentionally work at the kind of impact we have upon others. Quiet leaders recognize that for good or for ill, our interdependence means that people are never exactly the same after working with others.

Those who embrace interdependence are also more insistent on working towards win–win solutions. Rather than viewing others as competitors to beat, we view others co operatively and peaceably. We anticipate being able to work closely with them, and are willing to have sufficient flexibility to make this possible.

Other-centredness

Though we live at a time of rampant individualism, a consistent virtue of quiet leaders is their willingness to be other-centred – to be shepherding, servant leaders. The driver for decision-making is not personal comfort, but the good of others. Quiet leaders evaluate decisions on the basis of their impact on the lives of those they serve, not on their own life. People quickly sense whether they are being led by a leader who is in it for themself or one who has the good of the group at heart.

A common error is to view others as our alter ego. This is to see others as an extension of ourself, having the same tastes and wishes. The danger of this is that personal preferences then start to dominate the agenda – and are rationalized by the assumption that anything that we want is what the others would want – even if they don't yet recognize it. Quiet leaders should consciously make the decision to step out of the world of their personal preferences and fears to enter into the worlds of those they serve.

Thinking particularly of the other-centredness required of educators, Mark Strom writes:

> It has been my privilege to work with the leaders of a large public education system. I heard a little phrase there that I have come to hold dear: 'on behalf of'. I heard leaders use the phrase to provoke serious reflection on policies, strategies and initiatives. How was such-and-such a policy genuinely on behalf of teachers? How was a strategy

genuinely on behalf of schools and their communities? How was a pedagogical or curriculum reform on behalf of children, their learning and their futures? On behalf of. I have seen this little phrase marry care and wisdom.

In wise leadership there is always an 'on behalf of' to keep to the fore of our minds. It saves us from the parodies of leadership peddled by those who promote the cult of personality.

We find ourselves in a position of leadership: on behalf of whom? There are those whom we lead – the people within our organization – and there are those served by the organization as a whole. The school principal needs to think of her or his staff, and of the children they teach. Then there is the community in which the school is placed, and so on.[18]

It is when we ask the 'on behalf of' question and allow it to shape our actions and decisions, that we open the door to moving beyond a superficial version of success to actual significance.

From success to significance

It is helpful to distinguish between questions that ask what we *could* do and those that ask what we *should* do. Often our focus is on the former, with pragmatism as our driver. If we are to move from superficial success to genuine significance and lasting impact, the *should* questions need to dominate. From an ethical perspective, they are the logically prior questions. 'What should we do?' must precede 'what could we do?' This is not to suggest that the *could* question has no place – but it is not the opening question. Once we are clear as to what we should do, we then tackle the could options. If the conviction of what we should do is strong enough, we might well define what we could do more optimistically and coura- geously. Indeed, we might then have the moral compass required to embark on the journey from success to significance.

A leadership interview with Scot McKnight

Scot McKnight is a leading New Testament scholar well known for his work on the Jesus Creed. A professor of New Testament at

Northern Seminary, Chicago, he is the author of numerous books, and writes a popular but thoughtful blog which attracts over two million hits each year.

1. Scot, you have highlighted the significance of what you call the 'Jesus Creed' – summarized in Mark 12:29–31 as loving God with everything we have and are, and loving our neighbour as ourself. How might this help quiet leaders in their ethical decision-making?

One of your observations of the Hebrew midwives with Moses was that they kept the big idea, or the most important thing, in mind. Time and time again quiet leaders will encounter someone or a team leader and want to strike back, or take the short cut to the desired goal, or treat a person as a means to an end. The Jesus Creed of loving God and loving others as ourselves means each person in each situation must be given the dignity of respect, the genuine look in the eye with the impact of knowing that they matter – to the leader – regardless of who they are and what they can bring to the table. When we face a messy situation – as Bonhoeffer did with Hitler (surely an extreme example) or as a leader will when facing someone who seems driven to obstruct what the leader 'knows' God is doing – we need to step back and see the big picture: I am called to love that person, I am called to love others, and ask What is the most loving thing to do in this situation with this person and this group? The rules of deontology, the end of consequentialism, and even the character of the person must each be dipped deeply into the waters of the Jesus Creed. It will make a difference, sometimes the difference that requires more effort, longer patience, or deeper humility.

2. What temptations do you think leaders most commonly face?

Power. Plain and simple. Those who lead have the power to make things happen that they want to happen. So the temptation becomes this: to use the power we have to accomplish the goals we desire. Maybe then the biggest temptation is the leader's all too common situation of desire combined with power. Desire does not come off well in the Bible – it's that passion of will that does what the Ego wants instead of the self-denial that leads us to do what God wills. Here is where the gospel tells us more than we often want to know: the way of glory is suffering, the way of resurrection is crucifixion, and the way of victory is self-denial. In my life as a professor, and at times leader of our department, this has been the biggest temptation: to make my desires come into reality and how to get others to go along. Leaders shaped by gospel ask how Christ's life can be formed in them and in their churches.

3. How might leaders ensure they are held appropriately accountable for the power at their disposal?
By creating a gospel-shaped culture in which self-denial, love for others, and service mark the quiet leader himself or herself. Leaders create a culture by embodying their values and living out the virtues that matter the most. The apostle Paul surely created a church culture that was shaped by forward-looking, risk-taking encounters with the front edges of gospel work; he embodied – read 2 Corinthians 1 sometime – a kind of life that was open to the ever-new leading of the Spirit, and that is why his churches were so Spirit-conscious. Think of Jesus. Who could ever have passed by a sick person or a needy person – Peter doesn't in Acts – after watching Jesus minister to anyone and everyone? A culture not marked by the abuse of power is a culture shaped by a leader who serves, who lives under King Jesus, and who provides for others a cruciform life.

4. What warning signals might there be that an ethical dilemma is not being handled appropriately?
First, patterns. If a given dilemma occurs more than once and a leader acts the same way each time, and that action causes others some concern, then there is some evidence. Or if everything happening is always shaped in the direction of the leader's desires or someone else's desires, then we need to be concerned. Second, openness. Does the leader show signs of telling the whole story, truthfully, and without concern? Third, willingness to be corrected. A leader will tell the truth and be open to the best way forward. When any of these are not present, I'd be concerned with appropriateness.

5. Please pass on one key leadership insight you have.
The best leader is the best follower of Jesus. Our aim as Christian leaders is to indwell the gospel-shaped life of our Lord, and

that means that the leader is first and foremost a follower of Jesus. Leaders are tempted to see themselves in messianic tones. In an important book, Mark Allan Powell showed that when reading a passage in the Gospels, the pastor almost always identifies with Jesus while lay folks identify most of the time with the characters in the passage.[19] Not only does this habit distance pastors/preachers from their audience; it also encourages pastors/preachers to think of themselves – not as followers – but as saviours and healers and lords. Pastors will then need to develop the habit of seeing themselves as minor characters in the gospel stories in order to become better followers who, because they are following Jesus well, can lead others into the pattern of Christ's life for us today.

For reflection

The virtues of modesty, tenacity, restraint, interdependence and other-centredness do not exhaust the list of possible virtues, nor do they excuse us from thinking through the deontological and teleological dimensions of our decision-making. They are however key building blocks for leaders who make a difference not via charisma but by consistency, perseverance and working with integrity with others.

Spend some time thinking through your own life.

- What messy decisions have you had to make? What guided you in your decision-making – key principles and rules, or the desired long-term outcome, or some internalized virtues? Perhaps it was none of the above, or a combination of them. Looking back, what other options were open to you? What (if anything) would you do differently now?
- To what extent do you demonstrate modesty, tenacity, restraint, interdependence and other-centredness? Remember that as virtues they flow from who you are. If some do not come naturally to you, are there steps you can take to change this? For example, tenacity often grows when we challenge ourselves to stick to a decision and not to give up. We might not have started as tenacious leaders, but might find that we become tenacious.

- Think of some significant others in your life. What virtues serve as drivers for them? Which have you adopted? Are you satisfied with the outcome?
- In your setting, do you ever confuse could and should? If so, what would it take to refocus the question? Are you, as a quiet leader, willing to tenaciously work away at making this transition?

4

Discovering Your Voice: The Journey of Quiet Leadership

This, then, is what I have learned about how to change the world. As leaders we have ultimately only one tool. How we talk and listen – Adam Kahane.[1]

Quiet leaders as story-shapers

Leaders help to shape the stories of others. Be it through the circumstances they help to create in the workplace, the projects they birth or the new paradigms they introduce, each impacts the lives of others and therefore the way in which they experience their life. The decision to offer a promotion to a 25-year-old may open new doors of opportunities and adventure. At the same time the decision to promote the 25-year-old above the alternate candidate, a 40-year-old, might send painful signals to the unsuccessful applicant.

Some decisions are always difficult to make. A leader who decides to close down a factory and retrench the four hundred staff it previously employed, by that single decision alters the life story of four hundred families – more if one adds in extended families and friends who might be impacted by the retrenched person perhaps having to move to another city or needing to take early retirement or having to work significantly longer hours in a new job that pays less.

Because quiet leaders are conscious of the impact that their decisions may have on the lives of many, they are conscious of the responsibility that flows from being a partial author of the circum-stances that others find themselves in. They can never divorce their decisions from the faces of the people who will be influenced by them. In Chapter 2 we explored some biblical images of leadership – that leaders are servants, shepherds and stewards. All these images are relevant as we contemplate how to approach the leadership task.

To safely handle the power inherent in positions of leadership, it is important that leaders have a good self-understanding and insight into their own voice and journey. Because they contribute to the direction of other people's stories, they need to understand their own story and appreciate their own voice, lest it direct their decisions in ways they do not intend.

The decisions leaders make are often linked to their sense of vocation – the leader's sense of why they do what they do. At the less helpful end of the spectrum an inner voice might say, 'Well, someone has to do what I'm doing – so why not me?' while at the more constructive end there could be a clear sense of call to serve, to shepherd and to steward the people and resources that fall within their leadership brief. William Placher writes, 'Central to the many Christian interpretations of vocation is the idea that there is some-thing – my vocation or calling – God has called me to do with my life, and my life has meaning and purpose at least in part because I am fulfilling my calling.'[2] This sense of vocation or calling may dawn slowly – indeed, some reading this book may feel it too grand a concept. Quiet leaders, while not dogmatic about their calling, usually have a sense of a pattern emerging in their life – some-thing that helps them to make sense of the everyday. They recog-nize when something is inconsistent with that direction. In short, their leadership voice develops and they come to recognize what is harmonious with that voice, and what is discordant with it.

How then do leaders come to discover their voice? Some general reflection on the broad contours of narrative theory will provide some background to help answer this question.

The story we are: reflections from narrative theory

Our lives are filled with stories. Each time we turn on the TV we watch the drama of someone's life. While most TV programs fall outside the realm of both the believable and attainable, a growing genre sees the telling of more common tales. The communal lives of small groups of friends – be they the somewhat melodramatic interaction of *Coronation Street*, the bizarre *Six Feet Under*, the cynical *Desperate Housewives*, the winsome personalities in *Modern Family* or the amusing *How I Met Your Mother* – each is about the unfolding of life themes and stories. They deal with loss, betrayal, love, lust, intimacy, ambition, hope, death, family, work, play, money, cheating, birth, sickness, culture, country, place, being on the fringes, gender, friendship, fear, loneliness, acceptance, rejection, faith . . . in short, the major narratives of life. We watch because we sometimes sense part of our own story unfolding. Better episodes help us reflect not on the Simpsons but on our own journey.

The Christian faith is packaged in stories. During the modern era it became common to approach Scripture from a propositional perspective.[3] By linking one verse or theme to another, theologians tried to systematize the Bible's teaching and to formulate a set of doctrines that could be laid out in clear propositions. These proposals told us what should be believed, and by implication what should not. The approach is not without merit, but it meant that those parts of the Bible that did not fit neatly within the patterned schemes were often overlooked. Some of the most dramatic and moving parts of Scripture were relegated to the fringes – mere packaging from which no important propositions could be extracted.

The narrative approach to Scripture reclaims all the stories of the Bible. It strives to see the God encounter in the midst of the changing fortunes of life. It sits comfortably with the postmodern awareness of the complexity and ambiguity of life. Postmoderns don't expect God to turn up the same way each morning. They thrive in the difference and variety that is life and are therefore able to enjoy the rich tapestry of Scripture in a similar way to the ancients. Other than for arrogant modernists, who would think that God could be reduced to a set of predictable and precise proposals? And so we allow the narratives to sweep over and speak to us in life's varied seasons and settings.

Story is not limited to Scripture. In many ways human history is a vast collection of stories of what has happened to groups of people. More recently we have been alerted to the influence of those selected to be our storytellers. Now we listen more carefully to the voices on the fringe. And we have found some of those stories to be compellingly powerful. They have often shamed our trite glee in the supposed glories of the past. You tell the story very differently if you're the one who lost your land or lost the war! Likewise your recollection of what happened is likely to be very different if yours was the company that was taken over, as opposed to the company that did the takeover.

It is impossible to separate identity from story. Our communal, family and individual narratives shape the way we experience the world.

At its simplest, narrative approaches to leadership honour the concept of story, listen carefully to the defining stories of the leader's life and, if necessary, help in the rewriting of the script. Very different endings can result . . .

Narrative theory reminds us that every story is simultaneously like:

- Every other story
- Some other story
- No other story.[4]

As you try to discover your leadership voice it is helpful to pay attention to general principles that undergird all leadership, while also noting the idiosyncratic nature of your own leadership. Each of us is simultaneously like everyone else, like some other people and like no one else.

For example, you are like every other leader in having only twenty-four hours in each day in which to complete your work. And you are mortal. And you live in a fallen world where nothing is quite what it should be.

You are probably like some (actually most) other leaders in having to work within a budget, within an institution whose previous history imposes some boundaries on the journey you can tread, with staff who are not always ideal, in a political or cultural climate that poses particular challenges and limitations, and so on.

And then there is the intensely personal part of your leadership journey. While other leaders might not have some of the special resources that you do (perhaps you need only four hours sleep a night) and might not face some of your particular challenges, the overall configuration of challenges and resources helps to make your leadership situation unique. For example, though you need little sleep, you might also be a leader who has dyslexia, is subject to panic attacks and whose neighbour has a dog who insists on barking through the four hours that you would like to sleep! In addition, your life experience might include the break-up of your parents' marriage, a failed business enterprise (for which you still have debts to pay) and having lived in five other countries.

Spend some time using the three lenses set out in Table 4.1 to focus on your own leadership.

In These areas I am ...	
Like every other leader	
Like some other leaders	
Like no other leader	

Go back to the list over and over again. What are some of your leadership advantages? How can you use them to shape your leadership for maximum impact? What are your particular challenges?

How can you work with them to ensure that they are not your undoing?

While this exercise focuses on your leadership voice (singular), most of us are part of a wider leadership context, one in which there are leadership voices (plural). What are some of the special opportunities you have because of the people you know and are in relationship with?

Blocks to discovering your voice

One of the most common blocks to discovering our voice is to misread the difficult circumstances of our life as being unfair and unique. It is liberating to embrace Scott Peck's insight that 'life is difficult'. He starts his classic *The Road Less Traveled* with the words: 'Life is difficult. This is a great truth, one of the greatest truths. It is a great truth because once we truly see this truth, we transcend it. Once we truly know that life is difficult – once we truly understand and accept it – then life is no longer difficult. Because once it is accepted, the fact that life is difficult no longer matters.'[5]

Though this might sound like the first of the noble truths of Buddhism (life is suffering), the insight accords with the teaching of Christian theology. We struggle not because we are victims in a villainous world, but because we are humans in a fallen world. From a theological perspective, we live in the 'already and not yet' zone. Christ has come and redeemed us, but we still wait for the new heaven and the new earth envisioned in Revelation 21. Struggle is normal in this in-between time. Rather than paralyze ourselves with self-pity, we should embrace our struggles as a normal part of the embrace of life.

There can be other significant blocks. Being so impressed by another's voice can prevent us from exploring our own. In psychological terms, having an external locus of control rather than an internal locus of control can be an inhibitor. Sometimes we have fallen into the trap of naming ourselves as unworthy, or lacking in gifting. And so the list can go on.

Spend some time noting down any factors that may inhibit you from discovering your leadership voice. I've given an example in the first block in Table 4.2 – you then fill in the others. The list that most quickly comes to mind is probably correct. Now challenge each item you put in the 'why I can't' column. Ask if it really has to be this way . . .

Why I Can't...	Now challenge the myth ...
I can't lead beause I failed significantly in the past	Actually I learnt a great deal from that failure. There are now some things I will always do differently. My past failure has placed me in a far better position to lead sensitively in the present.

Discovering your voice

A Process

Though it may seem a little counterintuitive, people usually grow the most during times of struggle. This is certainly true for leaders. Naturally growth is not the automatic outcome of difficulty. Some problems see people crushed and unable to move beyond them. It is helpful to note a general life process that undergirds personal growth using the orientation, disorientation, reorientation cycle (Figure 4.1). I'll use a few psalms to make some comments about the pattern.[6]

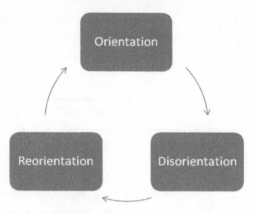

Figure 4.1: The orientation, disorientation, reorientation cycle

Orientation

In the orientation stage of life we believe that we have largely sorted things out. It is a stage where life makes sense, and we are content with who we are and our setting. We could see Psalm 1 as a classic 'orientation' psalm. Here the psalmist delights in a life which coheres and works. Those who follow God are rewarded, those who do not are like 'worthless chaff, scattered by the wind' (v. 4, NLT). The summary in verse 6 (NLT) is of a world that operates from the cause-and-effect principle and which is therefore just and fair: 'For the LORD watches over the path of the godly, but the path of the wicked leads to destruction'. In the journey of faith, this opening psalm captures where most of us begin. It is a stage of happy, optimistic, even naïve faith. The pattern laid down in Psalm 1 is most commonly true in life. Usually when we do the right thing, good things flow from it. However, what is usually true is not always true, and when the usual pattern of cause and predictable effect fails to produce the expected outcome, we can be thrown into a state of disorientation. Many factors in life are outside of our control, and when the tide of life turns it can be bewildering.

Disorientation

As life progresses, confusing things happen. Sometimes they are devastating. Certainty is replaced by questioning. The book of

Psalms may open optimistically, but Psalm 1 gives way to psalms that challenge and express confusion, even anger and rage. Psalm 13 (NLT) opens with the haunting question, 'O LORD, how long will you forget me? Forever?' while Psalm 22 begins in similar vein: 'My God, my God, why have you forsaken me? Why are you so far from saving me, so far from the words of my groaning?' In the disorientation stage, everything seems up for grabs. In the journey of faith, it is a stage where some abandon faith.

The stage of disorientation is critically important in personal (and leadership) growth, because it is a stage of seeking for deeper and more nuanced answers. It is a time to reject lazy or trite solutions. Sometimes it is a season when we realize that answers will not be found. We are often forced to face our own limitations – and the limitations of others. Those who embrace the experience of disorientation are usually able to empathize with others. From a leadership perspective, only those leaders who have undergone some experience of disorientation (even if only as a minor experience) are likely to be safe to follow, as it is very hard for those who have never struggled to understand and correctly 'read' the actions, fears and hurts of others. It is because of this that Henri Nouwen suggests that the best leaders are 'wounded healers'.[7]

Reorientation

Ideally disorientation leads to reorientation. As Psalm 126:5 (NLT) puts it, 'Those who plant in tears will harvest with shouts of joy.' Indeed, the book of Psalms concludes with a series of psalms of joyous praise. They have trawled the range of human experience but conclude that God is good. As the closing verse of the last psalm says: 'Let everything that has breath praise the LORD! Praise the LORD.'[8]

Reorientation does not mean that we live as though nothing troubling happened. It is a stage where we are able to keep moving in a positive direction even though we have suffered great hurt. It is the stage where our pain finds a settled place in our life – where we acknowledge it, but are no longer negatively shaped by it or defined by it. It is a part of our story – but it is no longer the only tune we are able to sing.

A spiral, not a line

The risk in speaking of 'orientation–disorientation–reorientation' is to think that this is a linear journey terminated after it has been travelled once (been there, done that, bought the T-shirt!). It's better to think of it as a spiral. Reorientation quickly settles to a more complacent orientation. It is not the same starting point as the initial orientation (deep experiences of struggle are not so quickly forgotten), but at some time the new orientation is likely to be unsettled by challenge and turmoil. Life is difficult . . . Personal growth is reflected not in our avoiding times of disorientation, but in facing each period from a starting point that is better rooted. Or to alter the image, the melody of our life never changes, but we are growing if what starts as being played with one finger is progressively accompanied by more and more instruments. What begins as dreary and dull develops into music that is majestic and moving.

I've stressed the importance of this process as it reminds us that leadership is neither a point that we reach nor a position that we attain. Both leaders and those who follow them are on a journey. The journey is rarely straightforward. From a Christian perspective, what we become (or are becoming) on the journey is of major significance. Leaders are willing to rethink their paradigms and face unsettling truths. They are quietly confident that disorientation will eventually lead to reorientation. Along the way they discover their own leadership voice.

In his book, *The Leadership Ellipse*, Robert Fryling discusses the paradox of the peacock.[9] This most beautiful of birds, so lovely on the outside, has a 'discordant cry' – a horrible voice. Fryling compares this to the dissonance between the inner and outer worlds of many Christian leaders. Outwardly the appearance might be pleasing, but inwardly our world may be full of turmoil and muddle. Owning our struggles, the orientation, disorientation and reorientation cycle that most of us go through, can be a path to ensure harmony between our inner and outer world.

Back to narrative theory

Culbertson has noted that 'We are born as storytellers who as yet have no stories. When we are born, we enter stories that began without us . . . [we are] a new actor in an old family script.'[10]

Although we are born into stories which began without us, and are greatly shaped by the circumstances and relationships that exist within our family of origin, maturing begins when we assume responsibility for the way in which we respond to the wider story of our life. While we are born into a family narrative, part of individuation involves our taking responsibility for the narratives by which we choose to identify ourselves. As we reflect on the stories that have shaped us, we should be alert to the possibility of alternate or multiple responses, endings and meanings. Alternate responses to the same initiating event can see very different outcomes. We are free to choose a meaning that is likely to lead to the writing of life chapters that we would like to live.

Let's make sense of this with an example.

A father of two boys is arrested and imprisoned for embezzling funds from his work. The first child interprets this as a 'shame' story – one which permanently marks the family as unworthy and as a failure. Not individuating away from the story, the family identity is accepted as though no other reading of the scenario was possible. The boy self-limits his future options by embracing this part of the family story as his own story. He lives life in the shadows because he does not feel worthy to live in the light of day. The story of his father has shattered his belief that he can write his own story.

By contrast the other son, while also deeply distressed by his father's imprisonment, is initially fuelled by a sense of rage. He senses that people are treating him differently because his father has been imprisoned. He feels the injustice of the situation – why should his father's mistakes shape his future? In speaking to his aunt she tells him of several other family members – many of whom have been very successful. He becomes intrigued by the range of stories in his extended family. Some are stories of success, others stories of disappointment, others of disgrace. He realizes that no one story can fully describe the family – indeed, he senses that each person has to write their own story. While he feels sorry for his father, he decides that he has another story to live. He takes steps to ensure that he does not make the same mistakes his father did. Born into a story that started without him, he now takes some responsibility for the shape of the story that still waits to be written and lived.

You might query the relevance of this for quiet leadership. In our opening chapter we asked why the tortoise usually wins. Remember Myrtle? She won because she had long come to terms with the fact that she didn't have much going for her. Indeed, in her race against the hare, her lack of natural speed was more than a small setback. Aware of the odds against her she set about doing what she could – putting one foot ahead of another, and that without grumbling, throwing a tantrum or morosely lamenting the unfairness of life. She chose an attitude – a voice – and it got her across the line first.

The voice we adopt in life will greatly shape the outcome of our leadership journey. It will also impact the way in which our leadership affects the lives of others. Our willingness to embrace the leadership voices of serving, shepherding and stewarding will help ensure better outcomes for those who decide that it's wisest to follow the lead of a quiet leader.

A leadership interview with David Crutchley

Dr David Crutchley is the Dean of the School of Religion at Carson Newman University in East Tennessee, USA. After many years as a missionary in Africa, David moved to South-western Baptist Theological Seminary, Fort Worth, Texas, which was then the largest seminary in the world, and where he was soon appointed Dean of the School of Theology. With the changing theological landscape at the seminary, Crutchley moved to his present post at Carson Newman, where he exercises a highly respected and influential ministry. No stranger to struggle and suffering, Crutchley has coped with a significant childhood illness and the death of his beloved daughter. He is well equipped to speak on the quest to find one's leadership voice.

1. What does vocation mean to you and how does it shape the way you embrace your leadership responsibilities?
Vocation is earthed in the soil of relationships. Meaning emerges out of the substance of life's journey and encounter with people. Leadership is a trust that calls for humility of spirit, simplicity of heart and generosity of life. The incarnation, crucifixion and resurrection define the Christian leader's task and calling: to roll up one's sleeves and to enter into the world where people live with shattered dreams and broken idols, to take up the cross of servanthood and compassion that leave us spent at the dusk of day, and to offer the daily bread of hope to those who travel with us along life's demanding road.

2. What are some of the key leadership lessons you have learnt during times of struggle?
In the midst of struggle leaders learn there is profit in patience: the urgent cry for resolution is often not forthcoming. Living with ambiguity and the burden of the 'why' is not for the faint of heart. Struggle clarifies priorities in our life narrative and tests our stamina and faith quotient. Framing honest questions in the struggle will require courage and risk. The voice of friendship and touch of family is critical for ballast in the storm.

3. Can a leader keep going when it feels like their world is falling apart?
It is hard to do life with a broken heart. It is difficult to show up when the poetry does not rhyme and the jagged pieces of life's jigsaw puzzle do not fit. My natural response is to want to hide, lick my wounds, and find a solitary place away from the burden of expectation and cacophony of life's noise. The depth of the crisis or the enormity of the struggle may require a sabbatical from routine and the demanding task of leading. Gradually, one learns to walk back into the circle of life and locate one's voice again.

4. If you were starting out on your leadership journey today, what would you do differently?
Guard against the following temptations:

● to give people access to your life at the expense of your family
● to expect to find peace with all parties

- to live burdened by people's criticism
- to seek to justify one's actions and decisions

Rather . . .

- own your mortality
- allow God to redeem your mistakes
- recognize that failure need not cripple but provides a platform for growth and depth of person
- understand that leading will inevitably hurt some other and we need therefore to lead gently and quietly.

5. Please pass on one key leadership insight you have.
The broken places and struggles in our lives help us to listen more closely to the stories of those around us and to see more clearly the signposts in people's lives.

For reflection

1. Spend some time reflecting on your own journey. Most people remember periods of disorientation. What precipitated a disorientation period for you? What did you draw from (or what are you currently drawing from) that period? If you have reached a stage of reorientation, in what way is it different from the original orientation stage?
2. Many narrative theorists suggest that we view our life as a book, with different chapter headings for each stage. What was the title of the last chapter in your book? And the present chapter? And the chapter you hope to write next? What do you need to do differently in this present chapter to ensure the next can be written to your liking?
3. How might your struggles make you a better leader? How might they help you to serve? And how might they impact the way you shepherd others? What difference will your struggles make to the way you steward the resources entrusted to you?

5

Challenging Our Excuses: Quiet Leadership and Character Development

The SHIFT test

Character is tested in leadership, especially as leaders have more power than those around them. By virtue of their leadership they have influence on the direction in which their organization will move, and often have the decisive say in the appointing, promoting and dismissal of staff. They help to determine the spending priorities of the organization, and are often instrumental in setting the salaries (or salary notch) of those employed – albeit that they do so within the constraints of the broader setting. On a day-by-day basis they often decide who gets which furniture and the brightest office, give the OK to work schedules and in multiple other ways are able to reward or hinder employees. Though guided by the policies of the board, most policies allow for a reasonable amount of personal discretion in their execution – and the leader's character is often most clearly displayed in the use made of that discretion.

While power can be abused, it is often not intentional abuse that is the issue. Often leaders are unaware of their *position power*, and that lack of awareness can make things very difficult for those who serve in the organizations they lead. Self-monitoring for fairness and justice is therefore important.

In this chapter we look at ways to work on and develop our character. Quiet leaders focus more on inner qualities than external charisma. The character question is therefore never far from their agenda, for institutions tend to take on the character and ethos of those who lead them, albeit that it may take a few years for the ethos to filter through.

Quiet leaders know that they are on a journey. While a major part of the journey is the strengthening of the organizations they are part of, they are conscious that the first port of call for change is their own character. Just as they commit to make the group they are part of the best it can be, they also acknowledge that they need to model the change they want to see. It is hard to be a quiet leader unless you are willing to challenge some of your excuses – the reasons you routinely give to justify the status quo of your life. The first step of courage that is taken is often a firm refusal to excuse your flaws, but to systematically face them and make the adjustments required.

It can be helpful to start with an inventory of where we are starting from. If we aim at nothing, we invariably achieve it – so we need to be clear as to the changes we would like to see occurring in our own journey of growth and character development. Perfection is not required but a commitment to personal growth is. It helps if we can identify some areas in which we are willing to interrogate ourselves. A good place to start is to take the SHIFT test, where we ask probing questions about our:

- *S*piritual well-being
- *H*ealth
- *I*ntellectual development
- *F*amily and Friends
- *T*ime and Treasure

Where we fall short in some areas, we should ask how we can shift from our present reality into our preferred option. Let's explore each in turn. The order is not significant as vulnerability in one area usually spills over into other areas as well. None can be ignored – though I will explore spiritual well-being more fully than the others, due both to its importance, and also to give an example of how to explore each area more rigorously.

Spiritual well-being

Our spiritual well-being is at the core of who we are. When we are in a right relationship with God, with others, with the created world and with ourselves, we are in a position to exercise a healthy leadership. There is a risk of overcomplicating what God requires of us. Jesus was willing to reduce the 613 Jewish laws to two. You find his summary in Mark 12:29–31, in what Scot McKnight aptly calls 'the Jesus Creed'.[1] It is worth learning by heart: ' "Hear O Israel: The Lord our God, the Lord is one. Love the Lord your God with all your heart and with all your soul and with all your mind and with all your strength." The second is this: "Love your neighbour as yourself." ' There is no commandment greater than these.

Allowing ourselves to be shaped by the Jesus Creed is our lifelong task. It will direct us to life-serving and liberating paths.

Sadly we need to recognize that faith can wear many unhealthy masks. For some people faith is itself the problem as it degenerates into toxic faith. While it might seem a slightly negative approach, it can be useful to identify what we should avoid. Peter Scazzero outlines what he considers to be the top ten signs of emotionally unhealthy spirituality as:

1. Using God to run from God
2. Ignoring the emotions of anger, sadness, and fear
3. Dying to the wrong things
4. Denying the past's impact on the present
5. Dividing our lives into 'secular' and 'sacred' compartments
6. Doing for God instead of being with God
7. Spiritualizing away conflict
8. Covering over brokenness, weakness, and failure
9. Living without limits
10. Judging other people's spiritual journey[2]

In recent years the tide has turned from assuming that Christianity was essentially good, to a widespread portrayal of the Christian faith as being essentially evil. Although this flows from some terrible caricatures, I think the topic is sufficiently serious for us to explore it at greater length. Quiet leaders will quickly realize that the development of their own faith journey takes place in a broader context. Part of the leadership mantle is to accept that we don't just inherit contexts within which we work – we sometimes need to strive to change them. Perhaps this is an area where a generation of quiet leaders who embrace a wholesome spirituality can help to transform the unhealthy and negative assumptions about faith that are currently starting to settle in the Western world.

So let's explore the problem more fully before applying it to quiet leadership.[3]

Religion is in danger of becoming public enemy number 1. Take this letter to *Time* magazine which was in response to an article on the singularity movement (crudely put, the article asked the question: 'Will computers become human?'): 'Although I will not be around to experience it, the idea of Singularity gives me hope for the future of mankind. Maybe they can program some humility into the superintelligent computer and it will find a cure for greed, poverty, disease and religion.'[4]

Without sidetracking onto the merits or otherwise of the article that led to this letter, consider the evils grouped together – greed, poverty, disease, *religion*. The growing antagonism towards religion is a trend we would be foolish to ignore. While we might be tempted to dismiss Christopher Hitchens' book, *God is Not Great: How Religion Poisons Everything*, as over the top and unfair, only the naïve would suggest that it has been without influence.[5] And it is simply one of a growing arsenal cited by what are now known as the new atheists.[6] The evangelical fervour with which they are approaching their task has resulted in a significant harvest; and, while the percentage of people who now claim to be atheist or agnostic is open to dispute, that the percentage is increasing is not. Even more disturbingly, while in the past atheists were usually content to justify their lack of belief in God's existence on the basis of purely *intellectual* objections, it is now increasingly common for that justification to be based on *moral* objections. To quote the title of Hitchens' book again, it is alleged that 'religion poisons everything' and is, in itself, an evil akin, as the *Time* correspondent claims, to greed, poverty and disease – a significant social problem to be obliterated if we are to attain a more utopian existence. While the famous G.K. Chesterton paradox claims: 'The Christian ideal has not been tried and found wanting. It has been found difficult;

and left untried',[7] a growing tide impatiently dismisses the sentiment as escapist and is unwilling to endure what they see as the poisonous harvest of religious faith.

That harvest is described in different ways, but ten common components (in no particular order) include:

1. Religious warfare
2. Colonial exploitation
3. Racial bigotry
4. The exploitation of women
5. Homophobia
6. The exploitation of the environment
7. Retarding the progress of science, with a particular focus now being on retarding the progress of medical science
8. Academic censorship with a resultant intellectual dishonesty
9. Intolerance of anything new
10. Hypocrisy

Clearly there is nothing attractive about this list, and if it is seen to be the normative result of religious faith, leaders who encourage their followers along a Christian path should expect increasing hostility to their message – presupposing they can find any potential followers at all.

David Kinnaman's study of the attitude of 16- to 29-year-old Americans towards Christians saw six recurring images.[8] They considered Christians to be:

1. Hypocritical
2. Interested in 'saving' people rather than in relating to them
3. Antihomosexual
4. Sheltered
5. Too political
6. Judgemental

Again, the list is far from winsome, and represents significant barriers to the likely receptivity to messages about the love and mercy of God.

Given this rather bleak landscape, and predictably the dismal perception of Christian faith in the Western world has been accompanied by a sharp numerical decline in those who claim to be adherents to the faith, we can ask if there is a future for the church in this 'after Christendom' era.[9] Perhaps we could be even more provocative and re-vision the question. If the harvest of Christendom was our poisonous list of ten (and I acknowledge that it is excessively one-sided to suggest that the list is fair),[10] is it possible that in the post-Christendom era a Christianity that more closely represents and reflects the teaching of Jesus might emerge? Should this be the case, the demise of Christendom might not be an occasion for lament, but one for celebration. Why would a quiet leader want to take their spiritual bearings from a faith that is so flawed?

For a more compelling vision of Christian faith to emerge, it is important that we recognize and renounce those elements of religious belief that leave us vulnerable to developing a toxic faith.

Before plunging into the unsettling question of what should change, let's acknowledge some of the positives that were accomplished in the Christendom era. It is only fair that we think of our achievements neither too grandly, nor too harshly. There is a glowing story of achievement that both can and should be told. Christians can claim credit for many of the positive social advances made in the last two thousand years. While multiple social factors are invariably at work in societal evolution, it is not fair to explore the abolition of slavery, the protection of the rights of women and children, the development of the welfare state or the shift in focus from retributive to restorative justice, without repeatedly referring to the Christian faith that motivated and inspired most of those who championed these causes. And they represent a small selection of an impressive array of humanitarian achievements.[11]

It would, however, be simplistic to assume the argument could be closed by referring to some of the more satisfying outcomes resulting from the interface between the Christ story and human history.[12] There is also a shadow side. There have been many times in the history of the church when it has been supportive of a right-wing agenda, which on occasion has revealed itself in racism, sexism, homophobia, militarism, ecological and economic exploitation, cultural insensitivity and more beside.[13]

Even if not actively supporting exploitation, faith can easily wear unattractive masks.[14]

So let's explore three masks which will have to disappear if a more authentic Christian faith is to be birthed in a post-Christendom era – a faith that can genuinely nurture and support quiet leaders.

First, there is faith as escapism. While it is perhaps understandable that African–American slaves longed for the day when the sweet chariot would swing low to carry them home, it is more difficult to understand why those whose lives are saturated with material abundance are sometimes so heavenly minded that they are of little use to those on the fringes of life, indeed those who are specially dear to the heart of God. In a post-Christendom era we must ensure that eschatology is used not as a crutch justifying escapism, but as a motivator of daring obedience. As people who have been privileged to see the end of the story, we know that ultimate victory belongs to the people of God. This should give us the courage to live in the light of God's coming kingdom in the present. Baptist theologian Stanley Grenz suggests that all theological construction should be eschatologically oriented – an important insight.[15] Allowing the future to guide the present could see a radically new form of Christianity birthed. Imagine, for example, if we truly lived backwards from the Pauline insight that the ultimate reality is that in Christ 'there is neither Jew nor Greek, slave nor free, male nor female, for you are all one in Christ Jesus' – to quote Galatians 3:28. This would indeed birth an infectiously different Christianity, one worth following in a post-Christendom era.

A second caricature left over from the Christendom era is that faith is often confused with the status quo. This mask bears no resemblance to what is required to be an authentic Christ follower, but nonetheless for many people things are good provided they've been around for more than twenty years. Nostalgia, rather than a commitment to a daring faith agenda, is the driver. Onlookers fail to find it inspiring. Perhaps we should stop thinking of ourselves as Christians, but as Christ followers. This is not a pedantic quibble. To stop viewing ourselves as static nouns and to introduce images of action might help to remind us that the Christian vision is of a daring journey of discipleship. It is a journey that does not bypass the cross and it is one that would never be undertaken without the assurance that resurrection follows crucifixion.

If any of this sounds like the status quo, then the status quo is not what it used to be!

Third there is faith as smugness and self-righteousness. While most have renounced the wagging finger, the image of Christians as people who see themselves as morally superior to lesser mortals and who tut-tut at the folly of those who don't share their faith, persists. That is not to suggest that we are people without a moral vision. However, in a post-Christendom world this vision is not proclaimed in 'Thou Shalt' terms. It is portrayed invitationally. It recognizes that it is one vision among other competing visions and that it needs to woo others by the winsomeness of those who have been captured by its contours.

These three false masks alert us to an important truth. Faith can spark life's loftiest journeys but, paradoxically, can also accompany and bolster its most misguided and tragic detours.

Because of the potentially abusive nature of faith it is important to highlight some of the warning signs that it is at risk of proving toxic. While an exhaustive list is beyond the scope of this chapter, danger signals include an insistence on unquestioning faith, or faith as compulsion instead of faith as invitation, or where there is legalism without love, or any form of faith that aims for power and control and attempts to justify the unjustifiable in the name of God. Indeed, simply alerting Christ followers to the possibility of toxic faith is a constructive start to the journey. Unquestioning acceptance of any who provide a Christian veneer to their agenda should be relegated to the naïvety of the past. Robust Christ following is the call of the day. Nothing less will persuade a cynical world to revise its negative verdict on the previous two thousand years of church history.

As this is a topic of such importance, I have cast it in a context wider than that of the individual quiet leader who is attempting to review their spiritual journey. Hopefully the wider context of the struggle for an authentic faith – one worthy of being named after Jesus the Christ – will capture the imagination of many quiet leaders as they become part of birthing a more hopeful future. At the very least, we should be willing to examine the outflow of our faith into life and into the organizations we lead or aspire to lead. We need to model an authentic and winsome faith – one which has been shaped by deep reflection on the teaching and ministry

76

of Jesus. Shaped by that message, our own spiritual life will be such that we are able to serve and shepherd others.

Health

Leaders, in addition to being servants and shepherds, are stewards. A key role of a steward is to look after the resources at their disposal and to use them well. One of the most fundamental resources we have is our physical health and well-being. Failure to be a good steward of our health is likely to see us underachieve in other areas as well. It can eliminate us from the race well before our time.

While it is unrealistic to expect every leader to have the physique of a champion athlete, a basic level of fitness is within the reach of most people provided they prioritize some time to exercise, and learn the art of saying 'no' to offers of second helpings of tempting, but essentially unhealthy foods. Once we develop these disciplines, they become part of who we are. When away from home, the quiet leader will remember that most hotels have a gym – and that it represents a good use of time to use the exercise bicycle and walking machine. Likewise we can educate ourselves as to what represents healthy choices from the menu – and will remember that being away from home and having the company pay the bill is not an adequate justification for ordering the cheesecake!

For some the challenge of remaining healthy is greater than for others. Life is not a level playing field. Some face major genetic challenges. Others have immune systems that crumble in the face of any new bug. Yet others need more sleep than average. We can only be who we are, and should realistically assess our starting point. Some will identify poor health as the most obvious challenge to their likely success, and will need to be active in ensuring the best possible outcome from their starting point. For others it will be an easier ride – with common sense and a little discipline enough to win this battle. This is not an area to 'tut-tut' about – or one where we should lament our misfortune if we are one of those who have to work a little harder to be healthy. One of the finest qualities of quiet leaders is their willingness to face reality and to move forward from it – this is so much more constructive than to endlessly sigh that we aren't as fortunate as others.

In short, better quiet leaders know their body mass index (and strive to keep it in the 20 to 25 range), keep themselves fit enough to remain focused throughout a long schedule, identify the health challenges in their schedule (such as having to travel a lot), and make a plan to deal with them. In doing so, they help to ensure that they are well enough to enjoy their journey of leadership.

Intellectual development

George Bernard Shaw is alleged to have quipped, 5 per cent of the people think, 15 per cent of the people think they think, 80 per cent of the people would rather die than think! Sadly there is probably more than a kernel of truth in this sentiment. Sometimes negative attitudes to learning are birthed at school, especially if students are forced to study topics they have little interest in. The attitude that learning is boring can seriously hinder future development.

Intellectual development requires more than taking additional courses or reading highbrow texts. It's a commitment to continuous development to ensure the insight, skills and clarity of thought to guide a group effectively. To do this quiet leaders need to be willing to move beyond the superficial and to expose themselves to different points of view, postponing judgement about them until after they are sure they have understood them fully.

Knowing the kind of learner we are is helpful. Some learn best in community – and love the back and forth of group discussion and exploration of a topic. Others prefer to shut themselves alone in a room as they devour one book after another. Others simply like to ask lots of questions as they go through life. Yet others learn by closely observing what others do and noting what does and does not work. Others learn by doing. Many find they fare best if they set aside about thirty minutes a day for some reading – if they give more time, their mind wanders, less, and it doesn't focus for long enough for anything to sink in. Rather than fight our learning style, we should co-operate with it. The key criterion is whether our world continues to expand. A danger sign is becoming increasingly set in our ways and unwilling to explore the new.

Setting modest goals is more likely to lead to success than striving for the unattainable. Most can manage a book a month.

While it's fine to watch TV and attend movies for entertainment, why not ensure that some thought-provoking fare is included in the diet? And maybe ask and allow yourself to be challenged by a simple question: 'What have I done or experienced in the last month that I have never done before?' At times the sheer pace of our life may make it necessary to extend the review period to three months, but start to challenge your excuses if you feel a need to make it longer than that.

Family and friends

When it comes to the crunch, family matters more than the work to which we feel drawn. Many have forgotten this, and have lived to regret it. Our children cannot delay their growing up . . . your 3-year-old will be 3 for a maximum of 366 days, but problems at work will continue to surface with monotonous regularity throughout your career. Life has different seasons, and during some stages it is wise to invest more heavily in family. At other times it is possible to give more attention to your career.

People often talk about balancing work and family life – and drawing up appropriate boundaries to demarcate each zone. While this has merit, it sometimes blinds us to the opportunities for synergy between home and work. If we are doing something we believe in (and why would a quiet leader commit to anything else?), our passion and commitment to our career can helpfully overflow into our family life. Provided their own needs are not neglected, children often catch the passion of their parents. Our spouse might enjoy seeing us engaged in something that matters to us. Provided we are also willing to listen to their story, they will often enjoy being included in our world as we recount our day and listen to their insights about it. It is when we refuse to talk about what we do at work that the great divide between work and home often arises. Feeling disconnected from what goes on in our workplace, our family resents its intrusion into the time we have available for them. When they are partners in the unfolding story of what we are doing, we expand their horizons and have a companion for our leadership journey.

None of this is to suggest that we don't take time to intentionally disengage from our daily task. Our work is a part of our family's story, but it should not be the totality of the story. Doing fun things together – things from which permanent memories will be birthed, is crucial for all of us.

Families can take many different forms. Many who read this might be single parents, or unmarried. The basic principle is that we need to be in supportive relationships outside of the workplace. Ironically if we are totally married to the company we will lose the windows on the world that we need to ensure that our organization remains fresh and life-serving.

Friends can also help us to keep perspective. Like family, they love us and accept us regardless of how we are faring at work. Remembering to diarize times to get together with friends is a very simple and sensible strategy to ensure the long-term enjoyment of life. Friends help us to remember that there is a world beyond our workplace. Honest friends help to alert us when we are starting to become untrue to our own self.

Time and treasure

Time and treasure are really two separate topics, but to spell 'shift' with a double t would annoy the pedantic! Let's look at each in turn . . .

Time

The question of time management is dealt with in greater depth in Chapter 10, but for our current discussion it is appropriate to include some comments on the relationship between time management and character. Leaders often have greater control over their use of time than others. They can chose to set a morning aside to investigate a new project or explore a possibility. Being in charge of one's time has many advantages but it also carries pitfalls.

One extreme is to waste large amounts of time. Accountability is often over the longer term rather than on a day-by-day basis. Leaders do not usually have to fill in detailed worksheets outlining how they used each hour. While a poor use of time eventually becomes obvious, it might pass unnoticed for a fair while.

The other extreme is to overwork. Again, usually no one is keeping a close record so excessive overwork may pass unnoticed for long periods.

How much work time is too much? One could argue that as the Hebrew work week was from sunrise to sunset for 6 days of the week, a 72-hour work week seems acceptable. Rather than being slaves to historic numbers, it makes better sense to ask how it was that they managed to work such long hours. A significant part of the answer lies in the rhythm of the work:

- A fair amount of it was physical, as opposed to our largely sedentary lifestyle.
- It often included family members and relatives working together, and long work hours therefore did not mean lengthy periods of the family being apart.
- There were not artificial stressors (such as heavy traffic).
- As there was not much specialization, most work was varied. Everyone had to be multiskilled. Job boredom and fatigue were therefore less likely to set in.
- Prayer and worship was built into the pattern of the working day.

Martin Luther's concept that we live *coram Deo* (in the sight, presence and awareness of God) is helpful. We decide the appropriate pacing for our life in the awareness of the God in whose presence we live. Leadership is not a job – but a vocation or a calling.

Theologians are also placing greater emphasis on the social nature of the Trinity. If God is Triune God or God in community, humans made *imago Dei* should reflect something of the communal life of God. The title of Stanley Grenz' book, *The Social God and the Relational Self: A Trinitarian Theology of the Imago Dei*, while initially sounding complex, gets to the heart of the matter.[16] A key part of being human is to be a 'relational self' or a being in community. Wholeness and self-care cannot be seen apart from the forging of relationships in community.

Finding the appropriate balance between work and rest, output and renewal, is important.

One helpful leadership rule is to distinguish between the short-distance sprint and the long-distance race. Often beginning leaders start as though they are on a short-distance sprint. They put everything into each task they tackle. In the end they burn out, or quietly withdraw from the race. By contrast, mature leaders learn to pace themselves. While they recognize that some challenges need sustained bursts of time and energy, they look to the overall balance in the work they do. They prioritize, and are content to leave some challenges to another day.

As a rule of thumb most people overestimate what they can achieve in a year, and underestimate what can be achieved in ten years. The secret lies in consistency of direction. The key to good time management is ensuring that effort moves in an unswerving direction. One project builds on the success of another and, as good foundations are laid, a tipping point is reached where the slow start gathers momentum and more significant gains are recorded. In a school, for example, putting time into developing a stable and committed staff team produces enormous benefits over time. Prioritizing staff morale and ensuring the ongoing development of staff might seem a modest start, but usually leads to excellent results.

It is interesting that the psalmist writes, 'Teach us to number our days aright that we may gain a heart of wisdom' (Ps. 90:12). Recognizing time as both a gift and as a limited commodity is essential for all leaders. It takes character to carefully evaluate the use of our time.

Treasure

A delightful but unsettling story from the fifteenth century recounts that a monk from a small village visited Rome to purchase a silver chalice to use in the church where he served. On his way home he linked up with a group of merchants both for company and safety. When night fell, he spoke about his journey and showed them the chalice he had purchased. Being merchants, they quickly asked what it had cost him, and when they heard the price they were amazed, for they realized that he had purchased it for well below its actual value. They congratulated him on his coup, and were delighted to think that such a modest and unworldly monk should have made so astute a purchase.

The monk, who had not realized the actual worth of the chalice, was stunned. In the morning he announced to the merchants that he was going to return to Rome.

The merchants laughed. 'Are you going back to buy more from the man who sold you this so cheaply?' they asked, thinking they had converted the monk to their capitalist ways.

'Oh no,' replied the monk, looking aghast. 'I am going back to pay the man who sold me the chalice the amount that it is worth.'

This is a wonderfully counter-cultural story. I have told it to many groups and usually get them to discuss whether they think the monk did the right thing. They rarely reach agreement! I've always been content to let the lack of consensus pass. Some questions don't have an obvious right or wrong answer.

While a self-review on how we use money would usually assess the plans we have to accumulate wealth, I'd like to include some more probing questions – questions quiet leaders should be willing to face. It is helpful to articulate our attitude to money. Many people operate without thinking through their philosophy on both making and using money. An important initial question is: 'Do I live to make money – or make money in order to live?' Muddling the two can cause great unhappiness, and while most would say they make money in order to live, you'd often be hard pressed to note it from their lifestyle. For many people, no bank balance is ever enough. Accumulation becomes more important to them than the responsible stewardship of what they have.

We should always be willing to ask who benefits from the financial gain of our organization. If the three dominant biblical images of leadership are of serving, shepherding and stewardship, we should be willing to ask how our wealth helps to further these tasks.

In the end it is not the wealth that we have that is the issue, but both what we intend to do with it – and what we actually finally do use it for. The difference between those who quietly get on with the leadership task and those who do not is that leaders are conscious of the resources at their disposal and the difference that these resources can make to the greater good they hope to achieve. They are willing to steward resources for the benefit of the vision they hope to achieve.

A leadership interview with Monica O'Neil

Monica O'Neil is the director of Vose Leadership, a highly regarded leadership centre within Vose Seminary, Perth, Australia. She mentors leaders and organizes professional development to help them face the challenges they encounter.

1. Monica, you're involved in training leaders. From your observation, what excuses most often trip leaders up?

The weight of external 'shoulds and oughts' often shout down the marvellous intuitions and leadership energy that sit quietly inside. So many surrender what they really see, hope for and dream of, to compliance with the norms, and the dreams and expectations of the usually unnamed powerbrokers who reside in their mind.

A second is that 'We don't have what it takes'. My response is 'Of course we don't'. I relate deeply to the ideas involved in a social understanding of the Trinity. We are designed for interdependence, to be among others in our endeavours, to contribute to common goals using our gifts, and that our lack of ability makes space for another.

A third involves a variety of blame games. 'Others did . . . others didn't . . . I never get/got a chance . . . I was robbed . . . I was betrayed . . .' Sometimes they are true, but even then we yield when we don't need to, blaming our lack of courage on external factors.

2. Of the SHIFT areas, which do you find the greatest struggle, and how have you moved forward in it?

Oh my goodness, it depends when you ask. I had found coming to terms with my own finitude a struggle. I naturally push limits, including my own. About ten years ago I hit my limits hard and found myself useless and a burden. As a non-contributor, I experienced being loved by God, Michael, my children and a few darling friends. That experience came as a gift in horrid circumstances. It was also augmented by some excellent mentoring and challenging counselling, exposing faulty beliefs, renewing my mind and transforming my life practice. I guess at core it was a spiritual well-being issue which played out in each of the other areas. I had to get off the throne and worship God. I continually have to monitor who I think is in charge of the universe. I do this with reflection on action in solitude and in the company of friends and skilled shepherds.

3. Any insight you can share about juggling the work–family balance?
Balance is such a weird word. I think my life is more like a strange canvas. I live most vibrantly when I have new colours and patterns coming onto the canvas. And yet I do not do well in a chaotic world. So I have developed some background patterns and habits which sit beneath the colours of the fresh and emerging things. These are routines such as regular family times (as our children are adults now), evenings at home with Michael doing familiar things, or time with friends. Sometimes work invades an area, and sometimes family or friends invade my work routines. My practices are varied, but intentional. While I pay attention to one area, I may need to return to a different part of my canvas to renew or refresh it or to just enjoy it a while.

4. People often say that leaders succeed because they are high in emotional intelligence. Is there a role for more general intellectual development?
Leaders are often endowed with intelligence in multiple areas. A commitment to a life-long disposition of curiosity and disciplined cultivation of our various intelligences is called for.

Being able to engage intelligently across multiple streams or portfolios in an organization is the result, simply because they can see more clearly the depth and breadth of an issue or a possibility. This capacity to problem-solve and engage complex situations with grace and wisdom comes from both the disposition and the discipline of learning for life.

5. Please pass on one key leadership insight you have.
Know what really matters to you. When it comes to the crunch of a bad day, resistance to change, outright opposition, a horrid interaction, a reversal, sheer boredom or an overwhelming success you can return to your centralizing point – who you really are and what you are really doing. A life lived in the light of God's love and surrendered to him in faithful service is pretty hard to knock off course.

For reflection

1. Overall, how did you fare in the SHIFT review? Where are you managing best? Is there an area you have neglected?
2. Does your faith help you to engage more fully in life, or is it a crutch that you escape with? 'What faith?' you ask. Why not rethink ways in which this could be a dynamic factor in your life?
3. OK – so what's your weight? Can you walk up three flights of steps without groaning? Is there something you need to do here?
4. Specify some things that you have started to think about in a different light in the last few months. Nothing to report? Then challenge the excuses that allow you to stifle your intellectual growth.
5. What interesting and fun thing have you done with either your family or friends (and why not both) in the last week? Nothing to report? Then make it the last two weeks. Still nothing to report? Hmmm. Who are you kidding?
6. Is there sufficient variety in your work week to sustain you through long hours?
7. What might 'numbering your days' to 'gain a heart of wisdom' mean in your context?
8. If money wasn't the issue, what would you like to do? Is it really money that is holding you back? Why not challenge that excuse?

Results Matter: Quiet Leadership and Optimizing Outputs

Teams that are willing to commit publicly to specific results are more likely to work with a passionate, even desperate desire to achieve those results. Teams that say 'We'll do our best,' are subtly, if not purposefully, preparing themselves for failure.[1]

When leaders are around, things start to happen. When good leaders are around, the things that happen usually move in a positive direction.[2] Leadership is about helping move individuals and groups towards desired outcomes. The outcomes can vary widely. Classically the good business leader is seen as one who helps the company attain optimal financial results for shareholders. The truly exceptional business leader is one who does this in a manner consistent with the vision and values of the company, while also developing staff and acting in a socially responsible manner. It is wise to assess the full range of outcomes (both intended and unintended) when assessing the success or otherwise of a programme. Often we look at the outcome in a single zone, and therefore declare something a success or failure on the basis of inadequate criteria.

Startling though it may seem, many organizations fail to focus on outcomes. Results are seen to be of secondary importance. While less common in business circles where generating a profit is crucial to survival, lack of attention to results is not unusual in not-for-profit organizations, some educational settings, and in religious organizations. Often they are reluctant to give a clear definition of what constitutes success and are therefore unable to specify whether they have achieved it or not. While hopeful that they are doing something of value, they reject specific indicators because they claim they overlook other important dimensions. So, for example, a church that has seen a decline in the number of people attending its services may claim that it is not overly concerned because the spiritual depth of the church has been enhanced. A school that fails to perform well in national examinations may dodge the hard questions raised by claiming that it refuses to teach with an eye on exams as that restricts the educational experience. While there might be a measure of truth in their explanation, it is a lot more credible when organizations announce in advance where their focus will be and stipulate the criteria against which they plan to evaluate their performance.

Some find a focus on results threatening. An inability to attain the targeted results might be seen as an obvious sign of failure, and a potential reason to have one's leadership terminated. It is therefore hardly surprising that some leaders like to stipulate vague targets – ones which can be massaged into a satisfactory shape should the need arise.

Quiet leaders know that results matter. While some followers go along for the ride regardless of the outcome of the journey, most want to know they are not wasting their time and that they have boarded a bus heading in the right direction. It is a matter of integrity for quiet leaders to be honest and transparent about what they hope to achieve. Because they have pondered the fable of the tortoise and the hare, they are aware that getting to the finish line is a result of successfully meeting multiple targets (one foot in front of the next) and they welcome opportunities to measure progress, even while they accept that a more (and sometimes less) ambitious finishing line might need to be negotiated. They also know that finishing one race is simply the invitation to commence the next.

It is one thing to acknowledge that results matter. It is another to think through strategies to increase the group's output – however it is defined. In this chapter we focus on enhancing the output of our leadership. We shall explore a particular model aimed at enhancing outcomes known as 'appreciative inquiry'.

Exploring *Appreciative Inquiry*

Appreciative Inquiry (AI) begins with the conviction that organizations are mysteries to be embraced rather than problems to be solved. In trying to enhance the outputs of organizations, AI adopts five generic processes:

1. *A positive focus of inquiry is chosen*

Rather than adopting the language of deficit or focusing on problems, AI focuses on the best aspects of the community and the hopefulness of what can be achieved. This is important if organizations are to find the energy to overcome inertia. A sense of defeat leads to paralysis, while a focus on positives empowers ongoing exploration and endeavour. Cooperrider, a key proponent of the approach, has written:

> In my own work in OD [organizational development] I have found that it does not help, in the long run, to begin my inquiries from the standpoint of the world as a problem to be solved. I am more effective, quite simply, as long as I can retain the spirit of inquiry of the everlasting beginner. The only thing I do that I think makes the difference is to craft, in better and more catalytic ways, the unconditional positive question.[3]

While it is possible to criticize AI for potentially glossing over the problems in organizations, it is better to start by focusing on what is working and life-serving in the organization. While problems cannot be ignored, the mental frame from which they are faced is important. The intentional choice to focus on positives must be noted. Facing problems square on as a first-step strategy often leads to organizations feeling overwhelmed and disempowered before they even begin.

2. *Stories of life-giving force are gleaned*

Stories give force to ideas, and provide hope of an alternate reality. They concretize the possibilities being spoken of. Uncovering life-giving stories is one of the tasks of the quiet leader. A natural inclination in leadership is to identify problems and to solve them. In this alternate approach we listen for the stories of what has gone right, and consciously cultivate them and give them a hearing. In doing this we help to create what Ludema calls 'vocabularies of hope'.[4] Hope is one of the most important motivators in life. The Bible is a story of hope, its final chapters confirming the delight of a new heaven and a new earth.[5] This confident portrayal of a wonderful future gives the courage to face the many difficult stages on the present journey. Some theologians see the concept of hope as being so important that they have built their entire theological system around it.[6] Recognizing this important principle, quiet leaders working within the framework of appreciative inquiry listen for stories that birth hope. They ensure that these stories get told.

3. Themes from the stories are identified

As multiple stories are told, certain themes emerge. These are usually the themes of what we do well – the strengths we can enhance and build upon. Knowing these strengths helps to secure our future. Quiet leaders remember that their group will succeed not because it stopped doing some things badly (helpful though that is), but because it did some things well. Spotting the areas we can succeed in is therefore essential.

4. Shared images for a preferred future are created

At this stage in the AI process we start to articulate what we would really like to achieve. Note that it is a participatory process. As people talk together, a picture emerges. It is not one person's creation. The quiet leader does not stand up and proclaim what the future will be. This is not to suggest that the quiet leader has no role in the formation of the dreams. To the contrary, people are usually part of the process because the quiet leader has already given some broad indication of the kind of journey that will be embarked upon. This starts to move the dream from broad brush strokes to a more nuanced and carefully articulated portrait. Naturally some flexibility will always remain lest one's dreams become a straitjacket. In summary then, as stories of hopefulness emerge, the group gives words to its dreams. Dreams which are jointly owned have a far greater chance of being realized. All become stakeholders in their being attained.

5. *Innovative ways to create the preferred future are sought*

The beauty of a group process in identifying desired outputs is that members usually come up with creative and helpful ways to move towards the preferred future. Often more than one strategy can be adopted. Mature groups realize that they might need to focus their resources and so adopt a single strategy rather than diversify. Provided that there is group consensus on the path or paths to follow, implementation becomes a matter of methodically working away at what must be done. It is at this point that our default fable is again relevant. While some groups get very animated by discussions on direction and possible outcomes, they can, after an initial burst of energy, like the hare decide that a snooze is in order. No results will flow from this. The quiet leader is realistic about motivation levels in groups, and is willing to work away systematically in the background to ensure that the group lasts the journey and remains focused.

Cooperrider expands on a four-dimensional cycle of appreciative inquiry for a life-giving organization. Imagine how each of these stages might unfold in your leadership setting:

- *Discover* what gives life in your organization. This is about appreciating what is.
- *Dream* about what might be. Here we ask what the world is calling for and begin to envision the impact we might have.
- *Design*, asking what the ideal design would look like and, from shared conversations, begin to co-construct in the light of what you have discovered about your dreams.
- Embrace your *Destiny*, sustaining your gains by empowering others, learning and making ongoing adjustments.[7]

The cycle repeats regularly. Adjusted designs help to create a new reality, so that when we resume the cycle we often discover that there have been subtle (or sometimes major) changes to what gives life in the organization. This ensures that dreams do not stagnate and that the organization remains dynamic and flexible to the challenges it faces and the opportunities it can embrace.

While the positive orientation of AI is to be welcomed, it should not be embraced uncritically. It certainly should not be understood to mean that problems or issues in a business cannot be noted or acknowledged. Failure to address a group's shortfalls will invariably hinder growth. However the ethos of AI is to ensure that we identify what leads to life in each organization. Too often the problems inherent in a group become overwhelming, and our instinct is often to pay the most attention to what is dysfunctional. If we pay attention to problems without a clear awareness of the positives we soon become dispirited and forget to build on that which brings life.

Some questions

1. What life-giving stories are waiting to be told about your setting?
2. Do you have a way in which to tell them?
3. If not, can you devise ways to ensure that transformative stories are told?

Identifying current outputs

If we are to enhance our organization's outputs, we need to have a clear idea of the base we are working from. Too often we operate with a vague sense of what our outputs are, and are content with generalities like 'the school year ran smoothly, staff retention rates were high, buildings were improved and academic results compared favourably with those of our peers'. Often we need to dig a little more deeply if we are going to enhance outputs. For example, while it is usually desirable to have high staff retention rates, there are times when turnover is desirable – not necessarily because current staff are unproductive, but because a fresh injection of ideas might be needed to avoid atrophy. So if staff retention rates are high, an output-focused leader may ask: 'How can we continue to retain staff while ensuring that we remain fresh, current and innovative?' A range of potential answers will spring to mind. Visiting other settings where good quality work is being done can serve both as a team-building exercise while also generating a raft of new ideas. Inviting the insights and input of an outside observer can also be transforming. We are often so accustomed to our own setting that we fail to see what is obvious to others.

We should also be willing to challenge our own publicity. Organizations are often praised on the basis of past performance. Helpful though this is, it might not reflect present performance. Sometimes groups are able to stay in cruise mode while they cannibalize the credit accumulated in the past. Occasionally there is a rude awakening to the changed reality. Groups that have a good reputation should be willing to ask, 'If we had no reputation from the past to help us, what reputation would our present performance be building for us?'

At some stage, we need to become specific. While birthing dreams is best done on the basis of appreciating the best of what we are and listening to our hopes and dreams, daily putting one foot in front of another depends on a willingness to note specific areas of drag and underperformance. The big picture will keep us motivated and hopeful. Attention to untied shoelaces that are tripping us will ensure that blocks to our dreams can be quickly dealt with.

A task

Why not spend a few moments identifying the 'outputs' in your current setting? Devise your own classification system (some areas you could consider include: financial performance; intellectual development; personal development; contribution to society; spiritual growth; cultural contribution, and so on) and then rate the current outputs against what you believe to be realistically attainable. If there are any significant gaps, these are areas where re-visioning is probably needed. However, don't forget to adopt the AI principle of focusing on the positives first. By first noting and valuing our strengths we provide the morale and motivation to work on areas of challenge.

Basic principles for enhancing output

We've looked at some broad principles for enhancing output. Now let's look systematically at some key building blocks of enhanced performance.

Know what you are trying to achieve

Move backwards from your preferred future. Ask, 'If this is what we want to become, what must we do now to get there?' In some settings outputs are more difficult to articulate and even more difficult to quantify, but it does not excuse us from the exercise. For example, though spiritual success may be an elusive concept for a church leader to define, don't avoid the challenge. What kind of church community would you like to be? What is the probable outcome from the steps you are currently taking? Are they the appropriate steps in light of the spiritual community you would like to be?

Focus on the strengths you have to achieve your goals

Goals will be achieved because of your strengths, not because of your weaknesses. Strengths therefore need the greatest attention. We should ask how they can be optimized. Sometimes strengths are in the 'almost made it' category. A little extra effort could see a tipping point passed where the strengths really start to work for you and the organization. Often strengths fail to achieve their potential because we don't give the extra 5 per cent of effort to ensure that they soar sufficiently high above the average to be noted.

Devise a plan to manage weaknesses

Though you will succeed because of strengths, weaknesses ignored or undealt with undermine your strengths. If there is something you cannot do, can you contract someone else in to do it? Do you need the insight of a consultant to help you identify blind spots?

Devise a strategy in consultation with all those impacted by it

It is extremely demotivating to be excluded from planning that will impact your future. People need to be involved in those things they have a stake in. Uninvolved employees will quickly succumb to a nine-to-five mindset. Worse still, they might passively (or actively) resist all change they do not feel a part of. Involve them in painting a vision of what can be done, and articulate how it can be achieved.

Break goals down into attainable stages

Some people quickly grasp the big picture. Others are more sceptical, and need to know what the next step will be. Regardless, no large dreams are attained without being broken down into attainable steps.

Celebrate successes along the way

Make the journey memorable for all involved. Usually organizations are on journeys that do not have a specific end point. However notable milestones might be achieved along the way. Opening the second, tenth or hundredth store in a chain is a milestone to be celebrated. Watching turnover pass the 100 thousand (or 10 million or 1 billion) mark for the first time is a cause to celebrate. The launch of a new programme at a local church, the sporting success of a school team, the academic success of our graduates, the promotion of a staff member – these and a thousand other triumphs can be causes for celebration. Celebration is the organizational lubrication that keeps friction at bay. It reminds us that what we do matters, is noticed, and contributes to the bigger picture.

One factor is worth developing more fully. Productivity comes through people. Most often God chooses to work through people, and the quiet leader is conscious of this. A truism is that people live up to the expectation placed upon them. If the leader views a staff member as a problem to manage, they will meet that expectation. However, if the leader trusts them and demonstrates that confidence, they will usually rise to that level of expectation. Peters and Waters write: 'Treat people as adults. Treat *them* as partners; treat them with dignity; treat them with respect. Treat them – not capital spending and automation – as the primary source of productivity gains.'[8]

Treating people well is not the same as 'mollycoddling' them. To the contrary, such 'protection' is patronizing and shows a lack of respect. It implies that we don't believe they can do any better. It is actually deeply insulting. We need to be willing to hold people accountable to clearly articulated and agreed-upon goals. The best goals include a 'stretch factor', and reward people if they meet them. Naturally quiet leaders do not agree on goals for their staff and then abandon them. If training is needed, they should ensure it is provided. They recognize that some people need more encouragement and feedback than others, and are willing to put systems into place to make this possible. They are conscious of their responsibility to ensure that each team member is set up to succeed, not to fail. They therefore ask, 'What does this person need in order to succeed?'

Peters and Waterman point out that people-orientated organizations have a tough side. When we move beyond hierarchy and introduce peer reviews, the reviews of highly motivated peers often reflect higher expectations than those accepted in hierarchically driven organizations.[9] Our own peers are often the strongest critics of our excuses. They know that it is not really that difficult. They sense when someone is in cruise mode, and if they have bought into the vision of the organization they are frustrated if someone is holding the group back.

In their examination of companies that boosted their productivity through their staff (as opposed to better machinery), Peters and Waterman identified three common factors:

1. *The language in people-oriented institutions has a common flavour.* Suggesting that form precedes substance, they argue that the successful companies they studied carefully crafted their language to create the reality they wished to achieve. Thus Hewlett Packard spoke about 'the HP Way' before it was clear what that meant, but as they repeatedly treated staff with

great respect, the slogan gained meaning. Other phrases like having a 'family feeling' or an 'open door' also started to gain traction.

2. *Many of the best companies view themselves as an extended family.* With many traditional networks struggling (for example, cultural societies, sports clubs, churches) people increasingly look to their workplace for support and meaning. If people enjoy being at work, they don't resent putting in extra effort. They aren't in a desperate hurry to leave at the end of each day.

3. *A rigidly followed chain of command is absent.* For information exchange, informality is the norm. Much is achieved via management by wandering around.[10]

A leadership interview with Haydn Nelson

Dr Haydn Nelson is the Senior Pastor of Riverview Church, Perth's largest church, and one which is highly regarded for its innovation, sanity, and willingness to work for the overall good of the church in Perth, Australia. During his time at the helm, Haydn has introduced many changes which have required courage and vision.

1. Haydn, you've had to raise hard questions about the effectiveness of some ministries you have been involved in. How have you found the strength to raise difficult questions?

Certainly some questions – and subsequent decisions taken – can be 'hard' in the sense of their complexity and their implications for people. These 'tough calls' do and ought to weigh heavily on a leader and will often require significant emotional expenditure. Strength for this type of leadership journey comes from different sources – most notably ensuring that you do not walk it alone and have alongside wise and trustworthy people. Yet, the empowering that really matters is undeniably spiritual. If a leader is deeply aware that life and leadership occurs coram *Deo* ('before the face of God'), then decisions and actions that you know to your core are honouring to Christ and in alignment with his vision for his church will always attract his empowerment and enabling.

2. How can leaders manage the juggle between really valuing what is, while also realizing that much needs to change?

Leadership must ensure that vision – that picture of the future that produces passion in the present – is clearly, compellingly and consistently articulated. Consequently, there is an inherent future-trajectory – a 'lean forward' – to wise leadership. This lean toward the future ensures that the tension between respecting 'what is' and yet hoping 'what can be' doesn't become mired in indecision and vacillation. Put another way, leadership needs to honour and respect the present (and the past) but *must be more loyal to the future*. This will require not only wisdom to know what needs to change but also a healthy dose of courage to do it.

3. Do results matter?

Yes, they do. It's sometimes commented that 'healthy things grow' with the obvious implication that something that is not growing is or is becoming unhealthy – that sameness may indicate stagnation. Without some form of measure, we may have no idea that a team/church/organization/event may have passed a point of momentum loss and is entering a decline or is moving away from its purpose. The church in which I serve has a statement by which we seek to measure not only current ministries but also new ideas – 'To lead people to Christ and build them into a worshipping community'. This simple statement of what we're about has been invaluable in guiding us to 'keep the main thing the main thing' and also guarding us against imprecision about what we're seeking to achieve. When a new idea or opportunity comes across my desk, I often find myself asking whether it will lead people to Christ and build them into a worshipping community. If it does either, then we'll actively consider it. If it does neither, we won't.

4. Can we be people-oriented and results-focused?

Leadership will always be full of tensions and paradoxes – and this is one of them. Indeed, the scriptural concept of 'servant leadership' and the scriptural admonition to 'speak the truth in love' (Eph. 4:15) are other examples. Certainly I believe that it is possible to value both relationship and results – but only when they are freed to mutually inform the other. Just as the speaking of truth must be informed by the command to love others, so also must the loving of others incorporate the speaking of truth to others. Consequently, being truthful about results or lack thereof does not presuppose a neglect of relationality but is a part of healthy relating. Indeed, using the New Testament model of 'truth-speaking in love', I would argue that being candid about results is a significant way by which we are kind in relationships.

5. Please pass on one key leadership insight you have.
I've learned that churches take on the shape, to a surprisingly significant extent, of the senior leader. I have seen this time and time again. This can be disconcerting at times, particularly for someone who may be described as a reluctant leader. Although reluctance in a leader may be a healthy sign of humility and a welcome corrective to selfish ambition, the dark side of such reluctance can often be a refusal to step fully in to who they are called to be and to do – and they remain a Saul hiding among the baggage (1 Sam. 10:22). Even reluctant leaders need to ensure that they are not holding their leadership too lightly. If God has called them to lead in a particular context, then they must step with confidence into that calling. Indeed, the fact that the church (or ministry, seminary or organization) begins to reflect their particular shape may be the very reason why God, in his providence, has called them to lead there.

For reflection

1. What implications might these principles have in your setting? If your staff spoke of 'your organization's way' what would they mean? What would you like them to mean? Do the two correspond? Could they?
2. If your organization is like an extended family, is it a functional or dysfunctional family? What holds your family together? What does it look like at its best? What are your family squabbles? How serious are they and are they solvable?
3. How accessible is the leadership in your organization? If an employee has a great idea to share, is it possible for them to get a hearing?

7

Casting Vision, Reshaping Paradigms: Quiet Leaders as Change Agents

In this chapter we explore the area that often comes least naturally to quiet leaders. Many tenacious, conscientious and disciplined people are not leaders. While observers respect their integrity and hard work, they fail to inspire because it is not clear what all their effort will achieve. Unless they master the art of developing and casting vision quiet leaders will steadily get on with their work, but they will not be leaders in the sense that they will not have followers.

The good news is that while vision-casting often does not come naturally, it is a skill that can be learnt. Often the simple realization that an organization needs an inviting vision of the future is enough to set quiet leaders on the right path. In this chapter we explore why vision-casting is important, how vision can be developed and how, if necessary, we can set about changing the paradigms within which people are operating.

Effective quiet leaders make a difference by helping groups change the way they think about things and by helping them to develop a picture of the future that motivates them and which they can work towards.

About vision and mission statements

To aid this it is common for organizations to have mission and vision statements. Sometimes the two are confused. Probably the clearest distinction is to say that our mission is what we do. It is our day-to-day business, and usually we aspire to do it well. Our vision statement captures what we hope will be the longer-term outcome of our action. A pain management company might therefore say that its mission is 'helping people living with pain to lead fulfilling lives' while its vision statement could be 'building a world where pain no longer matters'.

Vision statements are usually pithy, lofty and focused on a particular ideal. They express what we would like to happen as a result of our group doing what it does. They anticipate the future. Though attainable, it usually takes a while to get there.

Sometimes both the vision and mission might have a shorter-term focus. Let's say that you are committed to raising funds to build a community centre in your suburb – we'll call it Southvale. Our vision is then 'A community centre for Southvale' and our mission is 'raising funds for a community centre for Southvale'. Day by day our task is to raise the necessary funds for the project. The realized vision would be the built community centre.

Of course you might have had a loftier goal in building your community centre. You might hope that as a result of the community centre, crime in Southvale will be radically reduced, perhaps even eliminated. Your vision then becomes 'A Southvale free of crime'. In this instance, your mission of 'raising funds for a community centre for Southvale' has a purpose beyond the obvious.

In moving from a mission statement (what we do day by day) to a vision statement it is often helpful to add a 'so that' to the mission statement to help to clarify what the intended outcome is. In the example above, our fundraising group would then say, 'OK – so "our mission is to raise funds for a community centre for Southvale . . . so that".' The first answer might be, 'So that we have a community centre'. Someone might quickly object, 'but are we really building the community centre so that we can have a community centre?' Someone else then might reply, 'Not really. We all know we are building this centre to try and address the crime problem in our community. I'm really hoping that as a result of this we'll see a Southvale free of crime.' This could well be the 'aha' moment for the group as they realize that this is what they are really hoping for. Their vision has now been more profoundly articulated. They long for 'a Southvale free of crime' – they now have their vision statement.

It can be helpful to preface a vision statement with the words 'We see a . . .' – in this instance, 'We see a Southvale free of crime.'

The best vision statements inspire and motivate people. A leader without a vision statement has not yet indicated where the journey is leading. There is nothing for anyone to follow. Leaders usually have a following because people sense that if they put their effort behind this leader (or these leaders – given that leadership is often plural), they are likely to achieve something they would really like – and the vision statement is an important indicator of the direction the journey will take.

Naturally a vision statement parroted by a non credible leader will be dismissed. An inspiring vision statement, even when backed by a logical mission statement, cannot replace the virtues needed by quiet leaders. People look for leaders who display modesty, tenacity, restraint, interdependence and other-centredness. When these qualities are backed by a clear and worthy vision which is likely to result in a desired outcome, the quiet leader starts to find a following.

A word of warning about vision and mission statements . . . In the midst of the daily bustle, it can seem as though the vision statement is nothing but a useful and noble sentiment for the office stationery and website – a sentiment otherwise to be ignored. The pressing demands of the present prevent us from seriously evaluating what we do on a daily basis. Sometimes without realizing it we drift a long way from our vision. At times fundamental changes occur in society. Occasionally these changes are so fundamental that our daily mission is no longer likely to see us reaching our dream – the world we envisioned.

Quiet leaders remember to step back from the tyranny of the urgent, and run their activities through the grid of the overall vision and mission of their organization. They are proactive in helping to set and modify direction, rather than always reacting to the demands of the present. They know that the future is reached one step at a time, and that it is therefore important to check the direction of each step. In short, they put first things first.[1]

Working on paradigm change

How then might we embark upon the paradigm shift that ensures that we put first things first?

The term 'paradigm shift' was first used by Thomas Kuhn in his groundbreaking 1962 work, *The Structure of Scientific Revolutions*, and referred to a change in the basic assumptions within a ruling theory of science.[2] Kuhn argued that scientific progress was not evolutionary. Rather, after often lengthy periods of modest development and refinement, significant breakthroughs – scientific revolutions – occurred during which one conceptual worldview was replaced by another. Things are simply not thought of or seen in the same way after the paradigm shift has taken place. Though Kuhn limited his use of the term to the scientific realm, it has become common to apply the term far more widely.

For example, Guttenberg's printing press in the fifteenth century changed the way in which knowledge was disseminated. Books became smaller, cheaper and more readily available and thus knowledge spread quickly. While there were many refinements and advances in methods of printing after this 1440 start, the next real shift came with film, radio and TV – which made knowledge yet more accessible.

More recently, the internet has changed our paradigm. We now access knowledge and communicate with each other in a fundamentally different way. Imagine living in a world without email, Google or internet banking! Yet they have only been in the public arena for about two decades. It is a revolution that has been caused by the democratization of knowledge. We can check on our doctor's proposed plan of action to treat our asthma by consulting a hundred websites on the topic. Our physiotherapist's exercise plan for our troublesome knee can be compared with dozens of alternatives on the net. While we are usually wise to follow our medical practioner's advice, we have been empowered to ask questions about their decisions, and in so doing have ushered in an age of greater accountability.

Quiet leaders are involved in the realm of paradigm shift. They help their staff think about their roles differently. While we are using the concept of paradigm shift a little loosely, it can be argued that effective leaders spend time reflecting on what needs to change in each organization to ensure it meets its mission.

Sometimes the changes are dramatic. For example, many schools, despite their protestations to the contrary, are essentially staff-focused. Programmes are for the convenience of the staff and structured to ensure that their workload is minimized. Sometimes a major paradigm shift is needed to ensure that the school becomes student-focused. This involves a shift in organizational culture.

An example from my own group might help. I'm principal of a private tertiary institution. When I started, I was aware that many changes were needed. Some years back we introduced a can-dispensing machine so that students could easily access a range of soft drinks. One of the administrative staff members mentioned the machine in our weekly email to students and then added, 'Students are not to come to the office to ask for change for the machine.'

This seemed to me to be a teachable moment. I asked the staff member why students shouldn't get change from the office.

The reply came promptly, 'We don't want lots of interruptions.'

'But why are we here, and why does this office exist?' I asked.

'To help students,' the person replied.

'Then why are we so quick to tell them we aren't willing to help them?' I asked.

The staff member – who was basically an efficient and conscientious member of the team, suddenly realized that she was structuring the administration for the convenience of the staff, but in so doing was overlooking student needs. She immediately noticed the incongruence of this and another email was sent!

Institutional change comes when people start to recognize the need for such shifts. Leadership involves helping people to embrace change. People are often resistant to change unless they are convinced of its need by an alternate vision that motivates and inspires them. Part of the role of any leader is therefore to help create a vision of a preferred future – and to help others to see how this future can be reached.

How then can we help our group develop its vision?

Developing vision

Jesus' closing words to his disciples in Acts 1:8 are worth pondering: 'But you will receive power when the Holy Spirit comes on you;

and you will be my witnesses in Jerusalem, and in all Judea and Samaria, and to the ends of the earth.' He envisions a date, not far off, when, empowered by the Holy Spirit, this motley crew of followers would impact the world. It was a vision with a strategy.

Step 1: You will receive power
Step 2: You will be my witnesses in Jerusalem
Step 3: You will be my witnesses in Judea and Samaria
Step 4: You will be my witnesses to the ends of the earth

Given that the disciples' closing question to Jesus was, 'Lord, are you at this time going to restore the kingdom to Israel?' it was a pretty ambitious vision.[3] At this stage the disciples clearly didn't understand the heartbeat of Jesus and were still obsessing about the future of their nation, which at that time was under the oppressive rule of Rome, rather than the future of the kingdom of God. But it was a vision that came true! The Christian faith has spread around the world and continues to flourish two thousand years later because of the success of that improbable vision!

We've spent some time looking at the importance of developing a vision statement – but it is helpful to think more generally about vision and its importance for an organization. Vision itself is larger than a vision statement.

Bill Hybels suggests that 'Vision is a picture of the future that produces passion'.[4] In similar vein Nelson and Toler note that what differentiates a vision from a goal is the passion it engenders. They write: 'The biggest difference between a vision and a goal is one word: passion. A goal is like a dehydrated vision. It tells you intellectually what you want to accomplish, but it does not exude emotion or drive. Therefore it is not contagious.'[5]

Many argue that vision-casting is the key role of an effective leader. It is this topic to which we now turn.

Why vision?

In the first instance, vision is important because *vision leads the leader*.

Everyone needs a vision. Even if not leading a growing organization or doing something that will impact the world, we need to know where to pour our energy and how to direct our lives. John Maxwell suggests we ask three simple questions in helping to formulate a personal vision for our life:

- What makes you cry?
- What makes you dream?
- What gives you energy?[6]

It's worth spending some time answering Maxwell's three questions. It's logical to follow up by asking if the bulk of our life reflects our answers to his questions and, if not, how it could.

Let's now answer the 'why vision?' question systematically:

Vision produces focus

While vision always points to a range of things which need to be done and accomplished, it is also helpful in that it helps to *exclude* numerous energy-draining alternatives. Without vision it is hard to know what to say yes to and what to decline. When vision is crisp, decision-making becomes more focused. 'Does this help achieve the vision?' becomes the logical question.

A man digging a hole was asked why he was doing so. His reply: 'I'm digging the hole to earn the money to buy the food to give me the energy to dig the hole.' Without vision, life feels a little like that.

Vision ensures that the main thing remains the main thing

Linked to producing focus, vision helps to ensure that the main thing remains the main thing. It is easy to fall prey to doing the urgent but not the important. Without vision setting the agenda, everything starts to seem pressing. We put out one fire after another but deny ourselves the time to reflect and ascertain if we are doing what is genuinely important.

Vision increases energy and moves people into action

Much of this is at the level of the obvious. If you know that you are going hiking tomorrow you will get your pack ready the night before and wake up early enough to have enough time to walk the track. By contrast, if you have no plan for tomorrow, you'll probably watch TV till late and then sleep in even later.

Vision increases ownership

It is not fair to expect people to follow you if they have no idea of where you are heading. Vision is honest and up-front. It means that those who are following do so because they want to move in that direction and have a sense of ownership of what is going to take place. It gives criteria against which to evaluate the direction being set. It legitimizes – or delegitimizes – the path adopted.

Vision smoothes leadership successions

A vision is greater than any one individual. Too often when a group's chief executive officer resigns, the board scurries around to find a replacement from anyone who seems vaguely competent. Vision gives direction and helps to ensure that the next person is someone who will work to take the vision to the next level.

Some steps to take

John Maxwell claims that 'All great leaders possess two things: one, they know where they are going and two, they are able to persuade others to follow'.[7] So what practical steps can we take to develop a vision for our organization?

Pray and be proactive

One of the paradoxes of being a Christian leader is that we are simultaneously called to listen carefully to the leading of the Spirit, while at the same time we are called to be responsible stewards of the gifts and talents God has given to us. People often err on one end of this spectrum or the other. Some rush into action without prayer or thought; others, under the guise of close listening to God, refuse to do anything unless God sends several lightning bolts their way, and even then they want it confirmed one more time!

As a general rule of thumb (and there are exceptions) The character and shaping takes place. And nothing counts more than character.

With the backdrop of being continually shaped by prayer, Scripture and our community of faith, we then spring into doing; and as we 'do' we trust that the God who is shaping us is putting us in the places to which he has called us. In this way prayer and proactivity belong together.

In the first instance God has already guided us by the gift mix he has given us. If we believe in the providence of God, it is reasonable to assume that the context we find ourselves in is the one God has placed us in. Should he desire it to be otherwise, he will make it clear to us. With this knowledge and confidence we should not be afraid to be proactive in developing a vision of how God wants us to be good stewards of what he has entrusted to us in our context. The gift mix is not limited to those gifts we personally have. Quiet leaders constantly look to those in their orbit of influence. We might have neither the time nor the gifts to perform certain tasks, but if we can help others who have the necessary gifts to catch the vision, things will move in the right direction.

So the first step in developing vision is the confident awareness that something of value can be achieved in our context by the optimal use of the gifts God has given to us and to those within our setting.

An important psychological barrier to cross is from being reactive to proactive. Stephen Covey helps to highlight the difference between reactive and proactive language.[8] Ponder the list in Table 7.1 and see if there are any changes you might need to make.

Begin with the end in mind

Steven Covey makes the interesting point that all things are created twice.[9] Prior to a house being built, almost every detail is decided before one brick is laid or one nail hammered into place.

If we want to raise responsible students, we need to have that end in view or we may undermine it. If we want to help lead a school whose graduates become people of influence, we have to ask what such a school would look like, or our actions may work against it.

Reactive Language	Proactive Language
There's nothing I can do	Let's look at our alternatives
That's just the way I am	I can choose a diffeent approach
She makes me so mad	I control my own feelings
They won't allow that	I can create an effective presentation
I have to do that	I will choose an appropriate response
I can't	I choose
I must	I prefer

Table 7.1: Reactive-Proactive Language

An example from local church life may help make the point. Most churches say that they want a strong missional focus that will help people with little or no Christian background come to faith in Jesus. Yet they often then ignore that 'first creation' and do everything to retain status quo churches reflecting a Christian subculture that often dates to the 1960s or 1970s. Allowing that subculture to dominate cripples the likelihood of their being missionally effective. The vision is not being allowed to feed their actions.

The underlying principle is that we must begin with the end in mind and take steps that will help to attain that end. If we have a vision but then ignore it and don't allow it to shape decisions, it will not materialize.

Do the necessary research

While our vision statement is inspiring and lofty, when we ponder it we'll realize that it needs to be linked to tasks to be accomplished within a particular context. There is no short cut to doing the necessary research. If for example we have a vision of 'a world where children can flourish', and conclude that one of the steps we can take to help achieve this is to start an early childhood centre, we'll still need to check if there is a need for such a centre in our setting.

A key research component is a demographic study of the area. Make sure you check both the current situation and the predicted future trends. Of course future predictions are not foolproof, and areas can change rapidly. It is worth sourcing a range of opinions, and to plan for a range of alternate scenarios. It is helpful to identify other key players and resources in the area, and to find out their future plans. If our mission becomes 'recreating the wheel' it is not likely to inspire – nor is it likely to see our vision being reached.

Some things to remember about vision

Leadership consultant John Maxwell makes some important points about vision, noting that:

- *The credibility of a vision is often determined by the credibility of the leader.* Budding leaders sometimes need the cover or backing of an established leader to make their vision credible. Quiet leaders can extend their influence by observing emerging leaders and giving their backing to those they believe will make a difference. Being other-centred, quiet leaders are alert to those who would benefit from their support and backing. Likewise, they are not slow to ask for the support of other people of influence when they need it.
- *The acceptance of a vision is determined by the timing of its presentation.* Timing is crucial. Historians often comment on the role of timing both in the election of Jimmy Carter to the Whitehouse (after the Watergate scandal the public wanted a Washington outsider, which Carter was) and in his later loss after one term in office (the election followed shortly after the failed attempt to free American hostages in Iran). We are not always in control of timing – something politicians often lament. However, to the extent that we can influence the launch date of a visioning exercise, we need to carefully assess if the time is right.

- *The value of a vision is determined by the energy and direction it gives.* A vision without a 'stretch' factor usually leads to passivity and slow decline. We often forget this, and lament that staff don't seem motivated to give of their best. We need to ask if we have cast a large enough vision for them to be required to be a little more than they currently are. Some think that any vision is better than none. It is not true. A vision that is too small signals an organization without aspirations, whereas the absence of a vision can simply mean that a group on the move hasn't thought carefully enough about where it wants to go. When they do, even better things will happen.

- *The evaluation of a vision is determined by the commitment it engenders in people.* If there is no 'buy-in' to the vision, it will be dropped at the first difficulty. By contrast, vision that captures the imagination, if backed by competent leadership, will see high levels of commitment in people. Leaders should be realistic about the likely obstacles to a vision being reached. Most people are able to weather setbacks provided they have not been misled into believing that there will never be any.

- *The success of a vision is determined by its ownership by both the leader and the people.*[10] If only the leader is enthused by the vision, he or she will be a lonely visionary – but not a leader. Leaders influence other people. A leader without followers is a contradiction. Vision is therefore not proclaimed – it is developed in community and owned by the community. True, the leader often (probably usually) has a disproportionate role in helping develop the vision, but if it is only the leader's vision, a solitary journey will follow. While the entire community might not be actively involved in creating vision, enough of the key players need to be involved to ensure the credibility and trustworthiness of what is embraced.

Turning vision into action

Bill Hybels laments, 'I run across an alarming number of leaders who would rather *cast* vision than roll up their sleeves and attempt, with the Spirit's power, to *achieve* it!'[11] Later Hybels writes: 'Accomplishing a vision requires a lot more than pep

talks, slogans, emotional stories and heart-tugging video clips
. . . There's a huge difference between visionary leadership and
getting it done leadership.'[12] This is where the tenacity of the quiet
leader comes into play.

Before vision becomes action, it needs to be effectively communicated. Most groups have different levels of stakeholders. The
inner circle is likely to have been involved in developing the vision
– those less at the centre need to be convinced that the vision is
appropriate. If I had to suggest ten key principles in communicating vision I think I'd suggest these:

1. *Keep it simple.* Try to encapsulate the vision within one memorable statement. Think of simple ways to make it come to life.
2. *Know your audience.* You need to communicate differently
   with people at different ages and stages of life. If your staff
   team consists largely of recent graduates, you will be able to
   tap into their enthusiasm and idealism. A more experienced
   staff might want you to demonstrate that you have carefully
   investigated all issues, and will often need a longer 'lead time'
   before adopting a new vision. Likewise, some groups suffer
   from 'vision fatigue' where much has been promised in the
   past but little accomplished. They tend to listen to new vision
   with scepticism and to filter what they hear through past disappointments and hurts.
3. *Use stories.* People relate to the tangible but are suspicious of
   what might sound to be grand theories. Tell stories of what has
   happened in other groups who adopted a similar vision.
4. *Be vulnerable.* Tell why the vision matters and how it moves
   you. Let people sense your heart. If it appears to mean nothing
   to you, why should it mean something to others?
5. *Use multiple communication methods.* Some people are verbal
   in their orientation. They want to hear you speak about the
   vision. Some respond to written material. Provide it. Others
   need visual input – pictures and DVD clips are important.
   Others are influenced by knowing that key people support
   the idea – don't be the only one to talk but let opinion leaders
   express their support and enthusiasm for the vision.
6. *Have multiple entry points for involvement.* There needs to be at
   least one or two 'Oh . . . I guess I could do that' aspects to

a presentation. And having suggested them, don't forget to follow through and give people clear opportunities to sign up for aspects of the vision that they will help to champion.

7. *Affirm the vision over and over.* One presentation is not enough. People need to be reminded of it regularly. Many people have had experiences of a vision being presented with great enthusiasm and then being quietly swept aside when it proved too difficult. If we stop speaking about the vision, they will often conclude that this has been the fate of this vision.

8. *Update regularly on progress.* Regular updates assure people that we remain serious about what we are doing. They ensure that we remain accountable. They confirm that we are serious about the commitments we have made and that we are working towards them.

9. *Be candid about problems and difficulties while maintaining a positive and optimistic tone.* Most people are realists. They know that great things are not achieved without some struggle. When they know what problems are being faced, they are often willing to help, especially if they sense that the leaders remain optimistic about the journey and its long-term outcome.

10. *Show that you are committed to the vision and make it clear that you are doing all you can to make it come about.* Most people are reasonable, and simply want to be assured that the vision presented was not a seven-day wonder, and that the leaders are still on board and continue to believe it is a valuable and attainable vision.

There are other helpful principles. Leaders touch a heart before they ask for a hand. This can be done via building friendships, by journeying together with people, and by genuinely being other-centred. It helps to be part of the same community for a long period – perhaps even the bulk of one's career. Credibility grows with time. When people know that you are dependable, consistent and that you care for them, they are willing to care about the things that motivate you.

When we sense that a group needs to move in a new direction, it is important to win over the opinion-shapers first. If opinion-shapers are convinced by the vision, cautious followers and cautious sceptics (and about 68 per cent of people fall into these two broad categories), will almost certainly follow. That often involves thinking through people in our community one by one. Who are the opinion-shapers on the staff, on the board, among our clients and our wider community? We often need to spend time with them before we try to implement a programme of change.

At the same time, we should not be manipulative. If people have reservations, we should be willing to talk about them and face them honestly. Often the best visions go through a process of refining as people care enough to refuse to rubber-stamp them. In fact, if people say yes too quickly, it can mean that they are not really interested but couldn't be bothered to fight about it. They might not oppose the idea – but they also won't do anything to make it come true. That can then lead to one of leadership's loneliest places . . . where everyone has said yes but acts as though nothing is required of them.

Once vision is adopted, it needs to be refined with a strategic plan. The broad contours of a vision need to be supplemented with detailed planning. Failure to do this will leave the vision in the 'nice idea, but won't happen' category. Some of this links to the critical relationship between leadership and management – a topic we explore more fully in Chapter 10.

A leadership interview with Graham Hill

Dr Graham Hill is the director of a leadership centre jointly run by Sydney's Morling College and Tinsley Institute. An effective trainer of leaders, Graham is also highly regarded for his insight into the changing missiological landscape faced by Christian leaders.

1. Graham, what keeps you motivated and focused in your leadership? What do you hope your legacy will be?
Simple things keep me motivated and focused as a Christian leader. These include practising regular prayer, contemplating Scripture, reading widely, being coached and mentored, investing in emerging leaders, and being intentional about rest, recreation and relationships.

In addition to those simple, regular practices, I remain motivated and focused as a leader through intentional, ongoing self-reflection. Early on in ministry I decided to think critically about my values in ministry, my theology of ministry, and my particular ministry vocation and priorities. I want my values, theology, vocation, practices and priorities to align and to be coherent. These also need to be open to critique and examination in the context of my relationships in Christian community, my friendships and my family. It's in the midst of these practices of Christian discipleship, these habits of self-reflection and these immersions in human community that we discover our personal vision and vocation.

I hope that my legacy will be that I pointed people toward Jesus, toward his love, grace, holiness and transforming presence.

2. You're involved in training leaders. From your observation, how do people develop a vision for their own life?
Recently I taught a course called 'Exploring God's Call', designed to help people develop a sense of personal vocation and vision. In that course I suggested that all Christians are both leaders and disciples – in their homes, careers, ministries and relationships. Christian disciples are called to be leaders, in the context of the faithful use of their spiritual and natural gifts. They are called to be involved in ministries that use their gifts for the sake of Jesus' mission and community. Christian leadership is exciting and perilous, and is sustained by the development of a personal, particular vision.

Each of us needs assistance in becoming the leaders God has called us to be, and in exploring God's call on our lives. We develop a sense of God's vision for our lives as we explore biblical principles of Christian leadership, discipleship, vocation and discernment. We explore these biblical principles in our private study, within a community of faith and through participation in learning environments – college courses, Bible studies and other formal and informal settings. We develop a vision for our life through wrestling privately in our thoughts, that is, wrestling with our sense of call and personal vision. We also develop a personal vision through listening receptively to the honest feedback of others, through discerning our spiritual gifts and talents in the context of participation in Christian community, and through noticing the doors God is opening for service and ministry.

3. Can you identify some common mistakes to avoid when developing vision?

The most common mistake is trying to develop a personal, congregational or organizational vision in isolation. We need a dynamic, honest, caring community to participate in and to give us feedback. We need peer recognition and accountability. We need mentors who help us explore our sense of vocation. We need to experience various forms of resistance to test our growing sense of call – institutional resistance, personal criticism and other types of resistance. We need God-given examples in the Christian faith that show us the way of leadership, and how to lead with humility, integrity and vision. We need to read biographies of those who have gone before, demonstrating courageous servant leadership. And we need to develop a personal vision in the context of Jesus Christ's messianic mission in human history.

Another mistake is to develop a vision without attention to God in prayer and biblical contemplation. The best kind of vision is patterned after God's heart and is according to his will. This kind of vision can only be developed in an environment of sustained, attentive prayer.

4. How can a quiet leader, who might not have natural charisma or the ability to persuade from up front, successfully cast vision?

We sometimes assume that casting vision must involve dynamic, charismatic displays of personality, loud and up-front leadership behaviours, or the clever use of power. This isn't the case. While these things have their place, it is possible to cast vision and be influential in quieter, longer-lasting and more relational ways. We can cast a compelling vision of God's preferred future, both for individuals and organizations, through quiet leadership practices. These include sharing vision within the context of the development of deep relationships, and within the contexts of careful biblical exposition, the cultivation of healthy ministry teams, the prayerful transformation of conflict situations, the appreciation of diversity and difference, and so on. In short, these quiet leadership practices are about casting vision through cultivating a healthy organizational or congregational culture, and through demonstrating the value of that vision in your own life, integrity, service and personal values. This is vision-casting by attention to organizational culture, deep relationships, passionate prayer, personal integrity, and attention to the Spirit.

5. Please pass on one key leadership insight you have.
Be a Christ-centred leader. Allow the person, mission and vision of Jesus Christ to shape your leadership, and to determine any vision you commit yourself and others to. Read the gospels and ask, 'What was the vision of Jesus?' Absorb, appropriate and passionately communicate Jesus' vision.

For reflection

So what is your group's vision statement? And its mission statement? How quickly could you answer? If it took a while, there is almost certainly some work needed in this area. If the answer came quickly, do the statements still motivate and inspire you? If not, what should you do about it? And will you do what you should do?

8

What Others Become: Quiet Leadership and Helping Others Shine

A test of our leadership is what other people become as a result of being in our orbit. Good leaders bring out the best in people; poor leaders, the worst. Both Churchill and Hitler were leaders, but Churchill led Britain to its finest hour, while Hitler led Germany to its most evil. It is not just the outcome that was produced that mattered (the one success, the other failure), but the qualities that they each drew out from their people. Both played on patriotism, courage and the willingness to sacrifice, but Hitler led Germany to become a racist, oppressive society where the mean-minded and dysfunctional rose to the top, while Churchill inspired Britain to become a loyal, fairer and nobler society.

Leadership then is not just about getting a following. It is also about what people become as a result of following. We should aspire to be leaders who add value to the lives of others. Remember that unless you in some way mentor those who report to you, your role as their leader (or line manager) will be little more than being a policeman or a brake to them – you check on what they do or stop them doing things that aren't appropriate, but don't really add value to them. Mentoring is about adding value to those who follow our lead.

The term 'mentor' comes from Greek mythology where Odysseus asks Mentor, a wise and respected teacher, to look after his son Telemachus and oversee his development while Odysseus is away from home on a long journey. Mentor consents and exceeds expectations by the encouragement, guidance, nurture, love and support that he provides. As a result Mentor becomes the model for all subsequent mentors who guide the development of others by their willingness to share their wisdom and to care and guide those who look to them for their insights. While it is sometimes not practical for those in leadership positions to serve as a mentor to those who are directly accountable to them (this can lead to role conflict), they can nevertheless adopt aspects of the mentor's role by actively seeking ways to develop, nurture and stretch those who follow their lead.

David Stoddard and Robert Tamasy suggest that to help people reach their potential and to bring the best out of them, we need to help them to work on 4 Ps:

- Passion
- Pain
- Priorities
- Partners[1]

It's worth reflecting on each.

Passion

In bringing the best out of others, we need to take a little time to observe who they have been made to be. Some people light up at the thought of meeting new people or at being the main speaker at an event, while others shrink at the mere possibility. Some contemplate a night at the opera with delight, others shudder in horror at the mere mention of the O word! We've been made differently – and our differences reflect the humour, creativity and graciousness of God. A beginning principle in bringing the best out of others is to help them discover what they are passionate about – what they both enjoy doing and what they feel matters. When people know their passions and are able to work in areas they really care about, they naturally do their best, require little supervision and don't need constant motivational talks.

It is a principle that teachers know instinctively. I'm grateful to the Year 5 teacher who realized that my 'not interested in reading, not interested in maths' son was passionate about cricket. He didn't consider it to be reading if he flipped through a cricket magazine, nor did he think it mathematics if it was a calculation to see how many runs his side needed to win. By tapping into his passion and by linking reading and numeracy to cricket, his teacher was able to transform the situation in a very short space of time.

As quiet leaders, if we note the passions of those we are called to lead we will often be able to match some of the needs of our setting with the special interests and abilities of staff. It helps when we think of the passions of others as being legitimate requirements for workplace satisfaction. In other words ask the question, 'What will it take for Sally Jones to enjoy her work with us?' cheerfully, not resentfully, as though Sally Jones was making an unreasonable demand on the organization. This is a bread-and-butter question that every quiet leader needs to ask regularly for every staff member.

Too often we think only of the needs of the organization and desperately work at getting all bases covered, with relatively little thought given to the appropriate match and fit. Often the same job can be done in more than one way. With a little thought and a deep commitment to creating a pleasurable workplace, we can often find better solutions. Naturally every organization has many tasks that need to be done regardless of whether people enjoy doing them or not. Most people are philosophical about this, and are willing to undertake their fair share of such tasks so long as they know that some effort has been made to accommodate their interests. An old saying goes, 'Too long a sacrifice turns a heart to stone.' If people feel that they are simply used by the organization and that little attention is paid to their needs and desires, their attitudes will harden and they will be more inclined to do what's required, but nothing else. When a better job offer comes up, they will take it.

Sometimes people don't know what they are interested in. At times we might have to help people overcome some negative attitudes to work. One of the consequences of the fall was that work became a source of pain and struggle.[2] It would be hard to over-emphasize how tragic this has proved. Prior to the fall, Adam and Eve were assigned responsibility for the stewardship of all creation.[3] Work was creative, meaningful and productive. In naming the animals Adam helped shape the personality of the world in which he lived – for a name helps to define the essence of something.[4] Since the fall, work has been seen as a drudge – a necessary evil to ensure enough food on the table.

One of the purposes of Christ's incarnation was to reverse the effects of the fall. While this will be fully realized only at the dawn of the new heaven and the new earth, Christ's coming dents the present darkness. Those who follow him can hope for a sense of vocation or calling in their work. Ultimately we are called to do all things, be they small or great, in the name of Christ and for his glory.[5]

One of the tasks of the quiet leader is to internalize a redemptive attitude to work, and by so doing to allow their mindset to overflow into the lives of others. This might involve gently challenging a worker who assumes that work is simply the unfortunate interval between weekends. People often find work unpleasant because they expect it to be so. Quiet leaders model more hopeful attitudes. They believe that worthwhile things can be achieved by consistently working away in the same direction – provided the initial direction has been chosen with care and we find we are in the right race.

Once people have overcome their negative attitudes towards work, they can often see the creative possibilities that it opens up. Hopefulness and passion can be birthed. While Adam was called to name the animals, we may be called to name new projects or to usher in new dreams. Our passionate involvement can help to shape the contours of a new reality.

Pain

It is usually suggested that people work in the area of their strengths – and, when possible, most often this is sound counsel. However it is also important for people to face their shadow side as well as the pain within them. While we often project strength as an ideal and a goal to be striven toward, the Bible affirms that we are strongest when we are weak and when we allow our weakness to cause us to depend more fully on God's grace and strength. The paradox of 2 Corinthians 12:10, 'For when I am weak, then I am strong', is worth pondering.

Quiet leaders help to bring the best out of those they serve by creating an environment where hurt or weakness can be owned and where wholeness can be found, at least in part, by the entire team working together according to the principles of 1 Corinthians 12. In this chapter Paul teaches that, while we have different gifts, each gift is given for the common good. No one can do everything, but everyone can contribute something. Quiet leaders don't expect one person to be competent in all areas, but will find ways to ensure that the team as a whole covers all the appropriate bases. What one team member is unable to do, another might manage with ease. It is what we become together that counts.

We live in a fractured world. While few would dispute that in an ideal world children should grow up with two loving parents, happy siblings and the nurture and support of the extended family, it is an ideal that few experience. The resultant sense of loss can be agonizing. It is a loss experienced by many we work with – indeed, it might be part of our own story as well. It is not possible to lead a staff team without realizing the significant amount of pain that some carry. Often this is as a result of broken relationships, though pain can originate from many sources – not all children live longer than their parents; we might find that a cancer diagnosis is our own; our church community might inexplicably commit itself to self-destruction. Creating a transparent environment where people are free to own their pain, to name it, and to find ways to live more holistically because of it, is an important leadership role in the twenty-first century. Though it can be annoyingly trite if cited at an insensitive moment, the old adage, that 'all sunshine makes a desert', is true.

Wise leaders find appropriate ways to reveal their vulnerability. Sensitive self-disclosure backed with respect for the struggles of others usually leads to both respect and loyalty – as well as an authentic and wholesome workplace. Dealing well with people's pain will promote a far deeper level of trust than a jocular journey with their joy. Few people are difficult in cheerful moments – but the depth of our commitment to others is shown at times when pain is their close companion.

It often requires only minor programme adjustments to manage both sadness and delight. For example, in smaller meetings we can take a 'climate check' before we dash into business, and take a few minutes to catch up with how each person is. In larger meetings we can break into smaller groups to catch up with one other. In a setting with a clear Christian mandate, we can make sure that we allocate time to pray for each other. Where there has been conflict in meetings, we can ask for an 'emotional audit' at the end – acknowledging that we've had to deal with some difficult areas but asking each person how they are, and allowing an opportunity for people to dialogue further if this is needed – or we can set a time for such dialogue if immediate follow-through would prolong and deepen divisions.

Priorities

Many people struggle to prioritize, and so underachieve because they are easily distracted. Often people don't know what they are trying to achieve. Quiet leaders recognize that there might not be an exact alignment between the priorities of a staff member and that of the workplace, but can work with the staff member for an optimal harmonizing of both personal and organizational priorities. To be able to do this they need to know both what matters to the employer and what matters to the staff member. Ideally a discussion of priorities should take place before any staff appointment is made. This presupposes that the organization has a strategic plan that articulates what it is trying to achieve. Better to appoint a person who is a likely match than have to juggle with unmet expectations afterwards.

Most people are motivated by attaining their goals, and quiet leaders can bring out the best in others by helping them sift through their priorities and then setting attainable goals. We should set people up for success, not failure, so when people articulate unrealistic goals, we can help them structure a set of more immediately attainable targets. These don't have to be at the expense of lofty but less likely markers – some people are at their best when they face a major stretch – but each person should be able to tick off some items from their 'to do' list at regular intervals.

The meeting of priorities should be a cause for celebration, and most effective staff teams find ways to celebrate successes. An atmosphere of praise and encouragement, one where effort is both noted and rewarded, encourages innovation and participation. A simple test of performance in this area is to ask what positives have been achieved by the group in the last month and then to fill in the details of how these were noted and celebrated. If details prove elusive, we have probably forgotten to celebrate. It might be a good idea to make amends.

Partners

The first 'not good' statement in the Bible is found in Genesis 2:18: 'It is not good for the man to be alone.' This is a motif that extends beyond marriage. People fare best when they know that others are journeying with them. Best practice in both education and business is to ensure that staff members have access to mentors, and that peer-mentoring is also encouraged. Mentors are not experts who guide others from distant heights of success. Better mentors are fellow travellers, also committed to a journey of growth and willing to commit to our growth while also learning from us. Mentoring is a side-by-side journey.

Quiet leaders also pay attention to the interpersonal dynamics of the team. While a non-negotiable for effective teams is that all members must be treated with respect and courtesy by everyone on the team, it is only natural that some subgroupings of people work together more effectively than others. Where possible, we should group people with natural chemistry together, though we need to be alert to the danger of creating small cliques. This doesn't have to mean that every work team is made up of like-minded individuals at a similar stage of life. Often differences enrich people and make them aware of other dimensions to life. The quiet leader knows that the best teams are put together with careful thought, rather than simply being accidentally clustered together. Taking a little time to carefully plan who will work with who often saves more time in the longer term and leads to better outcomes.

Strategies for bringing out the best in others

With this background, let's look at some strategies to bring out the best in others. It has been argued that Jesus worked with three circles of people (see Figure 8.1):

124

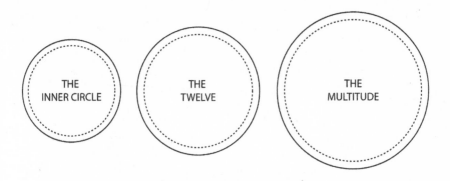

1. *The inner circle*: Jesus poured the most time and energy into the inner circle of Peter, James and John. He took them with him up onto the Mount of Transfiguration and was often in conversation with them alone.[6] Not too surprisingly, of the twelve disciples they are the three who went on to have the most influence.
2. *The twelve*: Jesus gave three years to journeying with the twelve disciples. In spite of their lowly beginnings, they went on to change the world.
3. *The multitude*: In his three-year ministry, Jesus was constantly interacting with the multitude. Some followed him fairly closely. Many of them made up the 120 who gathered for prayer on the Day of Pentecost.[7] Others had more fleeting encounters with Jesus. Some followed superficially, enjoying being fed one day but falling away when challenged the next.[8]

The principle is that *we don't work the same way with each group of people*. Before looking at how to bring the best out of each circle of influence, spend some time filling in the names of some of the people in each of those circles. You might have more than one inner circle if you find yourself in different settings (for example, your immediate family is probably at least one inner circle, but then you might have another of key staff at the workplace). Having concrete names and faces will help to focus your thinking.

My circles of influence

<table>
<tr><td>THE
INNER CIRCLE</td><td>THE
TWELVE</td><td>THE
MULTITUDE</td></tr>
</table>

....

....

....

....

....

....

....

....

....

....

The inner circle

The inner circle are the people you pour yourself into. You mentor them, and much of what you accomplish is done through them. Several factors go into developing your inner circle. They are likely to be people who have potential you can help develop. At the same time, they probably help to stretch and to develop you. A certain amount of chemistry is needed. Your inner circle can't be made up of people who drain and exhaust you. They are the people to whom you will pass on the baton of your own leadership. An inner circle doesn't always have a clear leader. It may be a group where everyone stretches and develops the others. It may be a project or leadership team.

There is always the risk that an inner circle becomes an exclusive clique. It is worth pondering ways to avert this danger. Being aware of it is a start.

The twelve

The twelve are more broadly based. If for example you are the principal of a school, the twelve would probably include members from your board, the school leadership team, other staff members, and younger emerging leaders. Much of what Jesus did he did informally. Through following and observing him, his twelve disciples learnt a great deal. The twelve are the people we remember to take along with us whenever we can – for good leaders travel with others whenever possible. Those who journey with us see the way we do things and can enter into our world. Wise leaders are open to some of the twelve finding their way into their inner circle.

Among the twelve was Judas Iscariot. Though a thief, Jesus let him be treasurer. The gamble didn't come off! There is much to learn from this. Clearly success is not guaranteed, but it is worth noting that the success rate was eleven out of twelve, a very pleasing outcome overall.

The multitude

The multitude or the crowd are all the people in our broader work setting. Jesus met their needs via teaching and was open to private conversations with some. Individual conversations can be life-changing. Think of Jesus' encounter with demon possessed Legion. Or the woman at the well. Or the man lame for thirty-eight years. Often we care best for those in the crowd by ensuring that we have structures that can meet the needs of others. Thus providing a solid system of pastoral care within a school, church or business is a far better way of caring for people than having the CEO rushing around trying to be all things to all people.

For all that, there are times when we need to stick our neck out and reach out to unlikely candidates. Take the Jesus–Zacchaeus encounter. You might remember that Jesus invited himself to lunch at Zacchaeus' home. Three facts about Zac? He was short, a tax collector and unpopular. And a fourth . . . He was curious, and climbed a sycamore tree for a glimpse of Jesus. Why did Jesus grace that unjust man's home? It was an unpopular decision with the crowd who made their displeasure clear. But when did Jesus let group pressure shape his decisions? The very people who complained loudest soon received a hefty tax return from a transformed Zacchaeus. I wonder if they had the humility to say, 'Thanks for not listening to us, Jesus.' Probably not, but quiet leaders sometimes need the courage to march to a different drumbeat.

Some general principles for bringing the best out of people

In committing ourselves to bring the best out of others, it helps to keep some general principles in mind. Here are my top fourteen:

Trust and believe in them

Many people doubt their own ability. If they sense that you share their doubt, they will be paralysed into inactivity. Quiet leaders turn the adage 'the good is the enemy of the best' around. Quiet leaders know that often the best is the enemy of the good as people see the best as unattainable, and are therefore not willing to even try. By affirming your belief that they can accomplish good things, you widen the canvas on which they paint.

While never naive, we readily affirm and place confidence in others. Theologically we know that all humans are made in the image of God. We are simultaneously created from the dust of the earth and the breath of God.[9] Dust alerts us to our limitations, the breath of God to the enormous potential inherent within each person. We should allow the hopefulness that we have for each human being to guide the way we interact with them. In this way we allow our hopes, rather than our fears, to shape reality.

Invite them to participate in stretching but worthy tasks

Too great a stretch and people snap, too small a stretch and they fossilize. Finding the right mix between the familiar and the new is an art. With time and reflection you will be able to differentiate between people who initially say no because they lack confidence – and therefore need your affirmation and encouragement to become more – and those who say no because they realize that something is genuinely beyond them. Likewise you will soon realize that some say yes, but act out no. Cultural background and an unwillingness to directly say no means that some will say a hesitant yes as a way to alert you to the fact that they mean no. Pick up on the hesitancy. Be honest with yourself as a leader. Is the invite purely about the good of the organization, or is this an invite that will help develop this person? At times it is only for the good of the organization. That pill can be swallowed more easily if we are honest about it – and candidly acknowledge that the organization is the one who gains the most. This does not have to be a disincentive. Budding servant leaders, like established leaders, need to have a servant heart. If they are not willing to put the good of the group ahead of self-interest, it could be that we are pouring our energy into the wrong person.

Give them space to do things at their pace (though don't abandon them)

Delegation is an art form. As a rule of thumb: delegate a task; give some space to achieve it; check on the progress; if satisfactory, give yet more space before checking again, and so on. Bill Hybels likes to quote the axiom: 'Performance buys freedom.'[10] If the person is not managing with the space given, work with them to find a better model. Often there is a small obstacle in the way. Some people need very precise guidelines as to what they can and cannot do, others appreciate the freedom to find their own path to the desired goal, and therefore just want a clear idea of the desired outcome. The best quiet leaders are flexible and adapt to the strengths and idiosyncrasies of the people they work with.

Set them up to succeed

Make sure they have the necessary training and resources. One experience of failure can sometimes undermine the confidence that has grown from multiple successes. People are often not rational in their self-appraisal. Many will be dismissive of their successes, but will mentally replay experiences of failure over and over again. Often people who do this have the sensitivity needed for organizational success, yet are the most at risk of dropping out of projects because of an unnecessarily hard self-evaluation when things go even slightly wrong.

Catch them doing things right, and praise them for it

The stereotypical image of the boss lurking around trying to catch a staff member playing a computer game or chatting on Facebook in company time has no place in the leadership style of quiet leaders. They believe in positive reinforcement, and know that it is far more valuable to catch someone doing something right than it is to catch them doing something wrong. While the latter cannot be ignored (though it should be understated, rather than over-stated), they actively seek for the positive.

Be on the lookout for kairos moments

Linked to catching people doing things right is looking out for *kairos* moments. The Greek idea of a *kairos* moment is that it is a timely, ideal or opportune moment – the very right time to say or to do something. Said at the correct time, some words can be transforming – said at another they might have little impact or prove offensive, or even be destructive.

Always give credit to people for what they have done

If staff members have played a key role in your success, *always* acknowledge it. Never forget to recognize their role. It is very discouraging for staff members to see the leader bask in the glory of what they have done, if their role is ignored. Quiet leaders always mentally ask themselves if they have thanked and acknowledged all the appropriate people.

Remember that you became a leader because someone trusted you with responsibility

Help make openings for others. The best quiet leaders ask if they should walk through a door that has opened, or if they should encourage someone else in the organization to try it. Nothing delights a quiet leader more than seeing a member of their team shine.

Celebrate success

Often organizations make the mistake of quickly dealing with errors and trying to find solutions to problems, but then barely recognizing success. This sometimes happens in schools where most of the attention is given to children who engage in disruptive behaviour. Subtly we convey the message that what gains our attention is failure. Not only does this demoralize (we are always dealing with problems) but also it means we don't provide enough reward to those who get things right. When we celebrate success, we highlight what people can aspire towards. If we do it well, it can be done in such a way that it motivates others to give of their best, as they will be confident that their efforts will be noted and valued. Celebration should not only be about the success of individuals but also about the success of the team.

Acknowledge problems and difficulties, and be candid in working for solutions

Celebrating success does not mean that we act as ostriches and refuse to acknowledge difficulties. We must be realistic in working with difficulties, while quietly conveying a gentle optimism that solutions can be found. A problem clearly stated and openly acknowledged is well on its way to being solved.

Don't harp on about what can't be changed

We all live within certain limitations. If something really bothers us or hinders us, we should carefully investigate if it can be changed. If not, we need to learn how to work with a reality we cannot change. At this point we have a choice to make. We can become bitter and negative because something is not as we would like, or we can simply get over it! The latter is far more constructive.

Laugh with, not at people

Laughter is the lubrication of life. There is a way of laughing with people that conveys a deep sense of affection, acceptance and good will. By contrast, there are ways of laughing at people that belittle and humiliate them. It is not hard to spot the difference. The writer of Proverbs insightfully notes that 'A cheerful heart is a good medicine, but a downcast spirit dries up the bones'.[11] Even when not naturally laugh-out-loud people, quiet leaders remember to smile warmly at others – it helps to set a tone of friendship and cheer.

131

Let them do better than you and take over from you when their level of leadership approaches your own

Leaders always find a place to lead. You need never be threatened by talent. It could be that the one whom you initially stretched and developed now helps to develop you. If they take your place, so be it. As a quiet leader your skills will always be needed somewhere, and there are lots of worthy causes. Sacrificial succession, where we hand over our leadership for the good of the group, is sometimes at personal cost but quiet leaders are philosophical about this . . . indeed, they are usually delighted. What better than that the group we so believe in is now being led by someone whose leadership eclipses our own?

Be a servant leader, constantly praying that God will show you ways to add value to the lives of those in your care

Remember the three S words that sum up the key biblical images for quiet leaders. We are called to be servants, shepherds and stewards. In combination, they are a powerful guide to our leadership. With a servant leader who shepherds those who follow and stewards the resource of the group responsibly, groups flourish and are able both to dream and to reach their dreams.

A leadership interview with Paul Windsor

Dr Paul Windsor was formerly the Principal of Carey Baptist College in Auckland, New Zealand. During his leadership the college underwent significant and effective change, growing rapidly in the process. Today he is an associate director of Langham Preaching, where he helps mentor and develop emerging preachers in the majority world.

1. Paul, you are involved in spotting and developing leaders in the majority world. What do you look for when you decide whom you will mentor and train?
While personality, skills and charisma have their place, my preference is to watch a person's manner and character. Do they listen

well? Is there a love for people shining through their eyes? Can they live in the footnotes, or must they be in the headlines? While these people may not immediately inspire, they are more likely to be the ones whom others will aspire to be like. It is placing this aspiration ahead of inspiration which helps me make these decisions. We may not want them to speak it out quite like Paul – 'Follow me, as I follow Christ' – and yet this is the quiet message which their lives speak.

2. Even Jesus had to cope with some leaders not turning out as he would have liked – Judas Iscariot the obvious example. How do you cope when people you have put a lot into disappoint you or go in another direction?
This is where leadership becomes like parenting. It is the same brand of love and disappointment that wells up within. As it is with children, it helps to choose to believe in people and have a vision of what they could become. People thrive in such a reassuring environment. When those with whom I have worked seek advice, I ask questions of them, listening and learning. But then I like to be more directive than reflective and let them know exactly what I think, before closing with 'but, if you choose to go in another direction, that's fine; I'll still line up behind goodness and mercy and follow you all the days of your life'.

At a key transition in my life, the great J.O. Sanders (author of *Spiritual Leadership*) was in my orbit and I sought his advice. But then I did not follow it. When I saw him next I mumbled an apology. He would have none of it, responding with 'but you've had guidance'. I found the clarity of his advice, in combination with the grace in his response, to be liberating.

3. How do you decide if something is likely to positively stretch someone, or negatively snap them?
As you have noted in this chapter, it helps if we remain in the world of their passion and vision, but also of their obedience. This latter point is critical as it opens up access to the divine resource which will want to facilitate stretching without snapping. Your earlier comments about 'servant–shepherd–steward' are also critical. This is the human resource which builds the necessary trust and gives people the confidence to take risks. But I find that two other S-words come into play: the sage and the seer. It is the art

of speaking wisely and boldly into peoples' lives. This is the best part of leadership, and when these divine and human resources are in play, it leads to far more stretches than snaps.

4. Any thoughts on developing leaders in a cross-cultural setting?
As I travel through different countries the same image returns. It is of a car with its various seats: the driver's seat, the passenger seat, and the back seat. In the colonial era the foreigner sat in the driver's seat behind the wheel and took control. To sit in the passenger seat (with the co-driver in a car rally coming to mind) is to speak of partnership. And then, jokes about back-seat drivers aside, the back seat is where someone sits quietly, helping and serving only when asked by those up front. To be effective cross-culturally I find that starting in the back seat is wise, with someone alongside who knows my culture and the nuances of the host culture. While it may be that I remain in the back seat, it is also a delight to be invited into the passenger seat. Effective contributions to developing leaders cross-culturally are best made from either the back seat or the passenger seat and without the ambition to be behind the wheel.

5. Please pass on one key leadership insight you have.
The God in whose image we are made functions as a team – and so should we. In Genesis 1 it was a team that worked on creation. In Ephesians 1 a team effected redemption. Here is unity, diversity, equality and multiplicity. Here is interdependence and relationship. Here is shared, and even rotational, authority. Leadership is about building teams made in the image of the Trinity. And then those teams go to work creating a place of belonging for everyone. You mentioned 1 Corinthians 12. I like to go even deeper into that passage, noticing how God, as the leader of the body ('But . . . God'; 12:18,24), designs the body to ensure that those considered dispensable are treated as indispensable and those without honour are granted special honour. People are far more likely to become all that they are designed to be if they know they belong in communities which are led like this.

For reflection

Before the interview with Paul, we looked at a list of fourteen principles for bringing the best out of others. Look over the list. Honestly rate yourself on each. In those areas where you are underperforming, identify ways you could change.

9

From Leadership to Leaderships: Getting Teams to Work in the Same Direction

Two key quiet leadership skills are the ability to bring the best out of others and to get people to work together to meet common goals. In our last chapter we focused on the former, in this one we look at the importance of developing strong teams.

Effective quiet leaders are surrounded by teams who work to ensure that the overall goals of the group are furthered. This requires more than groups of people working together happily. Quiet leaders keep an eye on outcomes, and regularly ask if the way in which teams are configured and the calibre of their interaction leads to the group meeting its goals more effectively. When the quality of the interaction among team members is not monitored, it can degenerate into competitive pettiness, cliques, time-wasting meetings and a multiplicity of agendas that have little or nothing to do with the group's overall mission and purpose. By contrast, when groups of people work harmoniously for common goals and are willing to monitor their progress in meeting these goals, the result is usually a stimulating and successful workplace.

Quiet leaders know that they are not omnicompetent. Conscious that there are many areas in which they do not excel, they are quick to acknowledge their dependence on the skills and insights of others. They recognize that successful groups have high levels of interdependence where drawing on the abilities of others is a normal part of group functioning. They therefore spend time reflecting on what helps people to work together effectively. They ask why some teams work well, and others do not. They develop the emotional intelligence to work both with individuals and with groups of people. If this does not come naturally to them, like Myrtle in our opening chapter, they plod their way forward, one step in front of the next, learning from both what works and what does not, and in the end they develop effective teams as they realize that without them even the most inspiring of visions will come to nothing.

Biblical reflections on teams

The concept of people working together is one that underpins the pages of Scripture. The individualism so prevalent in the Western world is foreign to the world of the Bible. Most of its narratives are about people working *with* and *on behalf of* others, rather than in splendid isolation, or for self-interest. Though the Bible declares that God is one, it portrays God in Trinitarian terms, finding no contradiction in the God who is Father, Son and Spirit being one God. As humanity is made in the image of God, it should reflect something of the triune nature of God if it is to be a valid reflection of God's image. While we are moving into theologically complex terrain, it is hard to see how a disconnected individual can reflect the nature of the God who is triune, or the God who was incarnated. In Jesus we see that God is God with us – or God in community.

Jesus developed his own team of twelve disciples. Though they were a motley crew at the start, they went on to change the world. By no stretch of the imagination were they a perfect group of people. While we quickly remember that Judas Iscariot betrayed Jesus, he was not the only problematic disciple. The gospels reflect many times of tension within the group. They argued about which of them was the most important and were reluctant to perform the mundane duties of community life – so much so that Jesus was left to wash the disciples' feet. Their stunning success, while a clear tribute to the transforming power of the Holy Spirit, is also a reminder that groups can make dramatic progress.

The apostle Paul had a clear commitment to working with others, and recruited co-workers for his mission trips, leaving behind dedicated teams of believers to grow the local church in each city he visited. These groups often left much to be desired, and some of Paul's letters deal with the significant problems that arose. In spite of their limitations, these fledgling churches had an astonishing impact on the ancient world. Paul saw the importance of different team members taking on different roles, and in Ephesians 4:11–13 writes:

> It was he who gave some to be apostles, some to be prophets, some to be evangelists, and some to be pastors and teachers, to prepare God's people for works of service, so that the body of Christ may be built up until we all reach unity in the faith and in the knowledge of the Son of God and become mature, attaining to the whole measure of the fulness of Christ.

In short, Paul sees a range of leadership roles (thus looking for leaderships, rather than simply leadership), and includes in his list apostles, prophets, evangelists, pastors and teachers. Each of these in turn helps to 'prepare God's people for works of service'. The circle of involvement grows wider and wider, but the common vision ('so that the body of Christ may be built up') does not falter.

While there is enormous potential in having people work together, quiet leaders master the art of getting team members to work together for common goals and shared dreams. Too often teams are made up of strong individuals who pull in different directions. Quiet leaders realize that while each person has their own abilities and aspirations, the leadership challenge is to get them to work together in such a way that the sum of the whole is considerably greater than the component parts.

The synergy that results from people working together effectively is enormous. Some of the older literature on leadership discusses long lists of leadership requirements. The focus is largely on one uniquely gifted individual rising above all others. This 'heroic' view of leadership is rarely attainable, and the inevitable failure to meet the full list of expectations often leads to a sense of guilt, while it drives others on until they burn out. It is both more realistic and more biblical to hope that the requirements will be met by a team than by an individual.

How then can we get teams to work in the same direction and thus to be more effective?

Two blocks to tick: climate and task

In an ideal setting people gather together as a result of shared vision and a common mission. They want to be together because they sense that they will be better together and more likely to accomplish dreams which they suspect will otherwise prove elusive.

Realizing dreams through teams is only likely to happen if the quiet leader can both ensure a harmonious, stretching, perhaps even fun-filled environment, while also keeping the group on task. There are thus two key questions that the quiet leader needs to ask. One is about the climate within the team, the second about its effectiveness in ticking off the tasks it needs to achieve. We focus on each block in turn, before looking at some of the areas of overlap between the two.

About climate

The moment we focus on group climate a raft of questions springs to mind. Are relationships good and harmonious? Do people feel free to offer their contribution, or do they remain silent for fear of being criticized or abused? Is there enough downtime in which members can laugh and imagine and discover the richness of the group's diversity? Do people yarn about their children and hobbies and relatives – indeed, the contours of their particular life, rather than just life in general? How is conflict handled? What is the trust level in the group?

There are some tangible things we can do to enhance the climate within a team.

Build unity, not uniformity

Unity means that a team is agreed on its vision, its purpose, and its philosophy or ethos. It is very hard to make progress unless there is agreement on these large building blocks.

It doesn't mean that everyone sees everything in exactly the same way, and certainly when it comes to implementing decisions, people often have very different work patterns. Initially this can make things seem difficult, even a little threatening, but quiet leaders allow for diversity, knowing that the team is

139

weaker without it. Uniformity in a team leads to blandness, and also usually results in significant blind spots – as a team where uniformity is stressed most commonly lands up looking at issues from the same angle, thereby remaining uninformed of the vista quickly spotted from a different position. Diversity in a team allows for different energy levels, capacities and ways of dealing with pressure and conflict. Ryan might cope with a difficult day by guzzling large quantities of cheesecake, and this might be to the astonishment of Anna who finds that a 10km run is the only thing that helps her de-stress. Quiet leaders don't try to control this diversity, but delight in it. Nor do they keep that delight to themself, but make a conscious decision to affirm the colourful quirks and idiosyncrasies within the team, thereby making them a strength rather than a weakness. Naturally everything has its limits. If one member's way of coping with stress is to scream at all the other team members, it is not really OK, and quiet leaders will work to help the person find more constructive alternatives.

Quiet leaders build harmony and unity within the team by consistently finding ways to affirm the contribution that each team member makes. They help others spot the positives in each person, thereby making it less likely that people will adopt the destructive strategy of always commenting on the negative.

This is not to suggest that there is no place for challenge in a team setting. Great teams have a teachable spirit. Although insecure people struggle with negative feedback and quickly become defensive, with encouragement and persistence this can change and issues which need to be addressed can be discussed.

Encourage real conversations

As a general principle, teams work best when they are places where real conversations are birthed. It is very frustrating to be part of a team that only works with the superficial. Leaders face facts. Sometimes those facts can only be understood after deep reflection. Few breakthroughs are likely to occur without it. Mark Strom writes: 'In my experience, when leaders do not foster a rich environment of conversation – an environment open to testing commitment and even to breakdown – a kind of void opens up at the very heart of the organization. This void is like a missing conversation.'

Quiet leaders encourage real conversations by participating in them openly and realistically. Instead of letting the team become trite or simplistic, they open topics up, giving a clear cue that genuine exploration of the topic is desired. This frees other team members to explore thoughtfully.

Distinguish between being aggressive and being assertive

Working teams are often made up of people who are leaders in their own sphere and it is not uncommon to have a number of forceful personalities within one team. Aggression is a behaviour that seeks to dominate others. It usually ignores the needs, opinions and feelings of others. Aggression intimidates and manipulates others and quiet leaders will quickly nip such actions in the bud, knowing that most people underperform in aggressive contexts.

Being assertive involves standing up for personal rights and expressing thoughts, feelings and beliefs in direct, honest and appropriate ways which do not violate another person's rights. Team members need to communicate openly, clearly and sensitively with each person being assertive and encouraging others to be the same. Part of being assertive involves a willingness to use 'I' statements and to own one's own feelings and responses. An example is: 'Can I be honest? The tone the group is taking is making me feel that I don't really want to be part of the conversation. When I hear raised voices, my instinct is to back away. But I actually care about what we are doing and don't want to opt out of the discussion just because, in my opinion, we are being a little bad-mannered.'

Some group members have a special knack of being able to defuse difficult situations with humour or affirmation or by depersonalizing the issue being explored. This is a very valuable contribution, and should be affirmed by quiet leaders.

Keep short accounts with other team members

Misunderstandings, miscommunication and conflict will inevitably occur in a team. While the line of least resistance is to adopt an ostrich-like stance and pretend that nothing is wrong, issues which are left to fester become more and more hazardous. If enough time lapses, attitudes which could have easily been remoulded set like concrete. A sign of healthy relationships is when team members have the freedom to talk honestly with other team members about hurts and misunderstandings. There is little point in working through difficult issues if you are about to leave a group, so a willingness to handle issues should be seen as a vote of confidence in the future of the team.

Teams lose their spiritual cutting edge and sharpness when hurt and pain are allowed to grow. A simple method to stop misunderstandings developing is to ask for a climate check at the end of each meeting. People can be asked how they are feeling after the meeting, and to give a rating of 1 (flattened), 2 (fine), 3 (delighted). You would usually expect 2s and 3s. A single 1 might be reason for the group to take some time to explore why, or the leader might follow through on it; several 1s should result in time for relationship-building being prioritized.

Encourage team members

It is easy to take team-mates for granted. It is also easy to slip into problem-solving mode, where the thing that has gone wrong gets all the attention, and we omit to celebrate our successes. In the end the team feels like it is only dealing with problems. Quiet leaders remember to tell the success stories. They link them to the names of team members so that they can bask in the praise of the group. If there are difficult things to be worked with, a team leader might say, 'Before we deal with the stretching stuff, let's remind ourselves of how much we got right, and of the things we can celebrate.' It is helpful to restate the positives again at the end. In short, it is best to start and end with a hopeful tone.

Say strong things with grace

Strong leaders can be very single-minded and strong-willed. Some people can be so full of truth they lack grace. They are so sure they are right that they feel justified in treating others critically, thereby losing credibility. Team members need to be both strong and sweet, full of grace but also full of truth.

Quiet leaders note the different way in which team members are able to receive feedback. Some people like things to be said directly, with no beating around the bush. For others, this is a sure trigger for defensiveness and counter-attack. An old proverb claims that 'a word to the wise is sufficient'. Many people don't need things to be spelt out, and find it humiliating when they are. For them a gentle pointer to a better way is enough.

Meet together regularly
Good working relationships are a prerequisite for an optimal team experience. While relationships usually build over time, the process can be hastened by the team spending time together. Team meetings should be a wholesome mix of business matters, practical details, feedback, evaluation, communication and consultation, mutual encouragement, socializing, spiritual formation, equipping, seeking God and maintaining the vision. The Pauline vision in Romans 12:15 of a community that is able to laugh and weep together should shape our interaction. Quiet leaders ask, 'Have we done what it takes to make it possible for us to laugh together and to weep together?'

About task

At an early stage a team needs to clarify why it is meeting. Is it a group for companionship and friendship, or are there more specific objectives that the group wishes to meet? While the goals of any particular team may vary, teams usually exist to enable a group to meet targets that an individual would struggle to meet on their own. Once we move beyond an individual working alone, questions of structure bubble to the surface. In the early stages of a team's life some key structural aspects need to be clarified. These revolve around the three key areas of authority (which should be linked to accountability), responsibility and decision-making. Unless there is clarity in these spheres, groups are unlikely to meet their goals.

Authority and accountability
If a group is to get anything done, people need to know who has the authority to make decisions and to enact them. We'll look a little more at decision-making later, but for now let's note that each team member must know which decisions fall into their brief – else chaos follows and either no action is taken, or you land up with ten people each buying the single lawnmower that was needed.

143

If people have the authority to act, they must also be accountable for how they use their authority. It needs to be clear whom team members are accountable to. A common mistake is to make people accountable to more than one person. This almost inevitably leads to confusion and playing one authority figure off against another. At times each team member is responsible not to an individual but to the team as a whole. While this can work well, very often when people are theoretically accountable to everyone, they are actually accountable to no one. It can be very awkward to look for accountability in a group setting, so teams often fail to follow through with underperforming members. It is better to discuss how this will be tackled before it has become an issue, so that the group's norms are transparent and easy to enact.

Realms of authority are often delegated. Thus at a school while the principal has overall authority (subject to reporting to the school board and the relevant educational authorities), large areas of responsibility are often delegated to vice principals. There are also subject heads and heads of year – each with specified areas of accountability. Principals sometimes make the mistake of intervening in areas that they believe need attention, without working through the designated staff member. This then undermines those who have authority in this area, which can sometimes lead to overt conflict – or hidden conflict (for example, in the form of apathy: 'Why bother? I'll be overridden'). We need to clearly ask and answer: 'Who are team members accountable to? What are they authorized to do?'

Responsibility
Linked to authority is the question of responsibility. Here we answer the question, 'Who is responsible for each team task?' In formal employment situations, written job or position descriptions are needed as without them people are unaware of the scope of their responsibility. They might also face unfair criticism over unmet expectations that were never clarified. Sometimes more modest projects are tackled in a team setting (such as organizing the school ball). Written job descriptions then become impractical, but the need for each team to know their responsibilities remains.

If we plan to hold people responsible for particular outcomes, they must have enough authority to accomplish the outcome.

The necessary link between these two is sometimes overlooked and results in a great deal of tension for those who are asked to account for outcomes that they were not empowered to influence. One of the most common ways this happens is when we expect people to achieve certain goals but fail to provide either sufficient time, staffing or funding to make the target attainable. In doing so we set people up to fail, rather than to succeed. Before holding people responsible for outcomes, quiet leaders remember to ask, 'Does this person have enough time, staff and finance to make this possible?' Sometimes other things might be needed – such as additional training, coaching or simply being affirmed and encouraged.

Decision-making

Team members need to know how decisions are made. Most commonly decisions are made in one of five ways:

1. The leader decides and announces the decision.
2. The leader decides and sells the decision to the team.
3. The leader presents issues and asks for ideas, then decides.
4. The leader and team raise issues and the team decides within boundaries which are set by the leader.
5. The leader allows the group to define the issues and decide.

Some groups consistently have one method for decision-making, though it is more common for a diversity of approaches to exist. This can cause confusion, unless underlying principles are explored. For example, a leader might usually allow the group to define issues and decide, but earmark certain areas as being for the leader to decide on. So long as the group knows what scenario exists and why, it is unlikely to be problematic. An inconsistent shuffling between systems leads to confusion. A common complaint is that sometimes the views of staff are welcomed and sought, that on other occasions staff input is clearly unwelcome, and that members can't figure out the rationale for the different approaches. In dysfunctional settings, team members are congratulated for taking initiative and being proactive in some situations, and then reprimanded for adopting a similar approach in another. This whimsical approach leads to a team that is mystified and apathetic.

Where the team is actively involved in the decision-making process, seek the opinion of each team member ensuring that everyone has a voice. It helps to detach an idea from the person making it. View any idea under discussion as the property of the group, rather than the individual. This is not to suggest that we should not thank individuals when they come up with great ideas, but that we stress the responsibility of the group to own all decisions made. We should not give some ideas an easy ride because they were volunteered by a popular group member, while others are dismissed because the person making it is cantankerous and difficult.

Decide which issues need communication and which need consultation

Precise boundaries of freedom and authority need to be decided. When a team member has been given authority in an area they need to communicate their decisions to the team only for information and clarification but not for discussion. A simple example might help. A team member has been given authority to organize the catering for a function. They should then report that the catering is under control (communication) rather than go to the team to ask if they would prefer chicken or beef (consultation) though in their report to the team they might choose to mention that chicken is on the menu (communication).

Consultation takes place when the team or team leader needs to be involved in the discussion and decision-making process. Consultation must then occur before the decision is made. Consultation is almost always needed when non-budgeted items are required or if a team member is in favour of a course of action outside the parameters outlined in their brief.

When team members report on issues it is wise to ask whether they are communicating or consulting. Sometimes team members simply want to be heard. They often face complexity, and knowing that others are aware of the issues they face can be liberating. If instead of being heard they are saddled with a long list of advice, frustration is likely to result and their 'note to self' will read, 'Don't bother to let the group know about the challenges I am facing.' Clearly this is less than helpful.

Reviewing decisions

Successful teams periodically evaluate and review their decisions. Sometimes teams sense that a poor decision has been made. Perhaps a marketing campaign is not going as had been anticipated, or a new programme may not be working as we hoped. We all know that there is sometimes a gap between what we long for and what is actually achieved. Unless a clear process is in place to review decisions, some teams dutifully work away at implementing decisions they know are flawed, losing heart as they do so, but unsure how to get the decision changed. Other team members might simply abandon the decision without consulting the team, simply protesting 'but it was obvious that it wasn't working' if called to account. Chaos is a small step away. When significant new decisions are made, a staged process of review should be put in place. It is usual to review at the early, mid and later stages of implementation. This is not to suggest that decisions should be second-guessed every time they don't bring instant success. We sometimes have to persevere with a decision before we will reap the benefits. However, just as teams need a clear process for decision-making, they also need a process to enable them to review decisions, and to modify or even abandon them if it is deemed wise.

RACI and CAIRO

A helpful acronym is sometimes used to guide through the decision-making process – RACI, sometimes modified to CAIRO.

RACI is a responsibility assignment matrix that helps us to answer who is *Responsible*, *Accountable*, *Consulted* and *Informed* when a specific project is undertaken. To expand briefly on each:

- *Responsible* answers the question, 'Who is responsible for this task or project?'
- *Accountable* clarifies 'who is ultimately accountable for the project?' The person who is responsible must get the project and its processes signed off by the person or group who is ultimately accountable.
- *Consulted* identifies whether there are other players or people with whom we should consult or collaborate for the project to be a success.

147

- *Informed* specifies who needs to be informed of decisions and actions taken.

RACI is sometimes expanded to CAIRO, with the O referring to those we *omit* from the process. It can be liberating for team members to know those things for which they are not responsible and that they need to feel no angst over. Likewise, if we are communicating with many people who do not need to be involved in a process, we often create an unnecessary workload and waste time.

When next your group decides on a course of action, make and check a RACI and CAIRO matrix. If you can't state who fits into each category, or if there is confusion and debate as to who fills each role, confusion and conflict is likely to arise. In short, until you can crisply and clearly fill in the CAIRO matrix, the initial empowering stage has not been completed.

Overlapping zones

Some issues have the potential to impact both the team climate and its focus on its task. Here are two areas that quickly impact both climate and task if mishandled.

Confusing principles with preferences

A principle is a fundamental belief. If the team contravenes a principle held by a member then it must address the issue and deal with the consequences. This is not common, but when it occurs, it can lead to hard questions. *Chariots of Fire* won the Academy Award for the best picture of 1981. Exploring the astonishing stories of the 1924 British Olympic team, one of the key issues it deals with is Eric Liddell's refusal to participate in the 100-metre heat because it was to be run on a Sunday. Liddell's deep religious convictions made it impossible for him to agree to race on the Sabbath – much to the astonishment of his fellow team members. For him this was a matter of principle and therefore, non-negotiable. Usually principles cannot (and should not) be altered.

Preferences sometimes parade as principles but they are no more than personal opinions. I have been involved in enough churches to see how the question of music and worship styles is often falsely dressed as a matter of principle when people are actually talking about their musical preferences. Describing the issue as one of principle makes the proponent feel that they hold the moral high ground. This is quickly exploded when it becomes clear that the matter is simply one of personal choice.

It is perfectly natural for teams to select the course of action that they prefer, but at times they need to be challenged to explore whether the path chosen is consistent with their principles. For example, many churches adopt programmes which are enjoyable to their members, but which are unlikely to help them to connect to the community they wish to serve. While they might claim that missiological relevance is a key principle driving their decision-making, the programme might demonstrate a commitment to the members' preferences, rather than to their stated principles.

The simple guideline is that while preferences can be overridden if they are preventing the group meeting its goals, principles should be respected and upheld.

Confusing critique with criticism

One of the key ways to grow is to receive feedback from peers. Team members should intentionally invite constructive feedback. The best forms of critique will acknowledge the positives, focus on things which can be changed (rather than those which cannot) and will view the person as a whole. It usually starts with recognition of strengths and moves on to areas of challenge. It is concerned with dealing with underlying issues and offers constructive ideas for development.

By contrast, criticism is negative, destructive and is focused on fault-finding. It often leaves a person feeling condemned and destroyed. Feedback without love and hope is criticism, which at best is unhelpful and at worst is devastating.

A leadership interview with Lucy Morris

Dr Lucy Morris is the CEO of Baptistcare, a large not-for-profit organization in Western Australia. Baptistcare employs well over a thousand staff members, and recently underwent significant and successful restructuring. Lucy is highly regarded for her ability to empower teams to work effectively and harmoniously.

1. Lucy, you have introduced significant (and successful) change at Baptistcare. How did you hold the team together during what must have been an unsettling time?

I worked out the bare bones of the outcomes I wanted for Baptistcare over a period of weeks, talking to people in other organizations and critical friends who had experience in change leadership. I was clear about which aspects of the plan I would consult on with my colleagues and which aspects people could make their own decisions about. The changes had to make sense with our vision, mission and values; including the timeframe that was available. I spent a lot of time telling the story from different perspectives, providing sufficient resources, appropriate authority, accountability loops and support. We celebrated the early successes, created a regular review process, and made sure the leadership team spent time together regularly on 'away days' to debrief and reconfigure the plan as we progressed with regular 'updates' and 'news' flashes. The clarity of the process and the reasons for the plan went a long way towards keeping everyone committed and engaged. I was also as open and enquiring as I could be, to reassure people they knew as much as I did and that we were working on this together.

2. Over 1,400 people are employed by your organization. How do you try to bring the best out of them?

We have committed to a significant range of strategies to recognize and value our people, which include annual values awards, quarterly newsletters with stories of achievements, challenges and learning, personal visits, a personal 'thank you', personal engagement with individuals, establishment of innovative career pathways and internal promotional opportunities, professional and personal development opportunities, training, education and leadership development programmes, flexible workplace arrangements to suit all types of family commitments, and all the leaders have the capacity to make arrangements to support people when in crises. This commitment never stops as we are always on the lookout for ways we can help support people and make their lives easier while working for Baptistcare. With approximately 90 percent of staff being women, we spend significant time strengthening and growing female leadership.

3. You work in the aged care sector, which in Australia is significantly underfunded. Presumably this means you can't reward staff with huge financial incentives. So how do you motivate your team?

We made a commitment we would aim to be in the top five paying organizations in our service sectors and staff know we value them and we will sacrifice other things to keep wages equitable. We see this as an issue of justice, given that women are traditionally underpaid and their work is frequently not valued by employers and the wider community. They are equal in the eyes of God and their contribution is equally valued, needed and essential for humanity to flourish. We also focus on intangibles such as access to career pathways, good professional development opportunities, training in leadership and governance, flexible work arrangements and making good use of technology, access to coaching, mentoring and critical friends. We also work to ensure that staff can see the difference they are making in people's lives as people come to work for Baptistcare for more reasons than solely financial imperatives.

4. When things go wrong, how do you stop the team spiralling into negativity?

We have regular reviews of our projects as part of our practice as a learning organization. We have four key themes for our daily work – leadership, innovation, quality and financial sustainability – and our reviews use these core areas of focus while we check our practices using the lenses of our vision, mission and values, 'to transform and enrich lives'. Together with a very strong sense of timeliness, we have 'learning conversations', using appreciative inquiry rather than leaving poor performance, unintended consequences or insufficient resources to strangle performance and outcomes. We're always focused on 'what could we do to help make things easier and better for our clients and our staff?' It makes the listening and learning from our mistakes easier to work through. And sometimes, we accept the awkwardness and imperfections and lack of achievement, because of individual circumstances.

5. Please pass on one key leadership insight you have.

It is impossible to be good at everything. There is so much I don't know. I recruit people into the team who are good at things I and my colleagues are not, who bring gifts we don't have and from whom I/we can learn. I look for people who could do my job when I leave as I am only writing a 'chapter', not a book. These are also people who have wisdom, insight and courage, who can give hope, who love learning and who are open to making mistakes. I don't want perfectionists; I want people who love other human beings as unique in the eyes of God. I want people who will stretch themselves, learn, weep and laugh as companions on our organizational journey, who will leave us richer and who will themselves be changed positively by their time with us.

For reflection

Patrick Lencioni has suggested that teams are often held back by five areas of dysfunction:

1. Absence of trust
2. Fear of conflict
3. Lack of commitment
4. Avoidance of accountability
5. Inattention to results[2]

In one way and another, this chapter has considered each of these pitfalls, but it helps to group them together under one heading. As we conclude this section, quickly evaluate the teams you are part of. Evaluate the health of your teams in the light of the five spheres Lencioni discusses:

1. Do your teams have a high level of trust? If so, how was it built and can its success in this sphere be duplicated elsewhere? If not, is it just that insufficient time has been given to building group relationships, or have there been some destructive trust-breakers? If something happened to break trust, what can be done to restore it?
2. How does the group handle conflict? We look at this more fully in Chapter 10, but is conflict avoided at all costs and if so, why?
3. Are teams members committed to the group's mission as well as to the group members? A commitment to both is usually

unbreakable, while a commitment to only one can see a group member switch allegiance ('I can accomplish this just as effectively with another group').

4. Then there is the accountability question. Are people held accountable? Are they given sufficient authority for the accountability to be meaningful?

5. Do results matter to your team? What are your team results? If you struggle to answer the question, is it possible that this is a realm of inattention?

10

Beyond Dreaming:
Quiet Leadership and the
Management/Leadership Juggle

People often distinguish between leading and managing, often making a virtue of the one and negating the importance of the other. However leadership that is not rooted in and supported by good management usually results in little more than daydreaming, while management without leadership leads to impeccable but irrelevant structures.

Warren Buffet has memorably suggested that management does things right, but leadership does the right thing. Banks and Ledbetter suggest that:

> Management is about coping with complexity – it is responsive. Leadership is about coping with change – it too is responsive, but mostly it is proactive. More chaos demands more management, and more change demands more leadership. In general, the purpose of management is to provide order and consistency to organizations, while the primary function of leadership is to produce change and movement. Management is about seeking order and stability, whereas leadership is about seeking adaptive and constructive change.[1]

In the Bible we find examples where leadership was needed and others where management skills were required. Exodus 18 records that Moses' father-in-law Jethro taught Moses the key management skill of delegation when Moses was in danger of becoming swamped with the daily detail of dispute resolution. Moses – who like many quiet leaders was reluctant to assume the mantle of leadership – had succeeded in leading the Hebrews out of Egypt. With God's help he moved them towards the new reality for which they were destined. These are classic leadership outcomes. But without Jethro's management expertise he might have landed up burnt out and unable to continue. The account serves as a reminder that leaders and managers belong together.

Because the focus of this book has been on leadership, this chapter aims to balance this with a focus on four management skills that are needed if quiet leaders are to be effective. As is generally true in leadership, the key is not necessarily that the leader has all these skills, but that they recognize their value and ensure that there are those on the team who implement them effectively.

The four skills we'll focus on are:

1. Time management
2. Running effective meetings
3. Delegation
4. Conflict resolution

Though I suggest that these are management issues, there are areas of overlap, and any attempt to tidily and categorically differentiate between leadership and management is likely to be a little forced.

Time management

Time is a level playing field. We each have 60 seconds in the minute, 60 minutes in the hour, and 24 hours in the day. True, some of us have more energy than others, and some will live to be 104. But on a daily basis, we all start with 24 hours. How we fill them makes the difference between our lives being more or less extraordinary.

The Ecclesiastes 3 principle is that there is a time and a season for everything under heaven. Remember that when we say, 'I don't have enough time' or 'I wish there were 25 hours in a day' the Bible quietly disagrees. Part of good time management is finding the appropriate rhythm of life and time.

Good time management remembers the Sabbath principle. One day a week we must delight in being unnecessary. The world can somehow muddle along without us at least one day in seven. It is sobering to remember that the Jewish day is considered to begin at sunset, not sunrise. 'There was *evening*, and there was *morning* – the first day' (Gen. 1:5) – it was not morning then evening. In other words, we begin in the place of quiet reflection and sleep. Only then are we equipped to move out into the day. It is a wonderful model of grace before works . . . We receive rest before we have done anything to deserve it. This helps guard against becoming puffed up and conceited. Instead of rushing into the presence of God proclaiming, 'This is what we have done', we enter thankful for what God has done.

In the Bible two Greek words are used for time, *chronos* and *kairos*. *Chronos* refers to clock time. Meetings are scheduled in the realm of *chronos*. We say that the meeting will start at 3.00 p.m. and finish by 4.00 p.m. What happens in that hour of *chronos* may be dull or mildly interesting, but every now and then something more dramatic takes place. We sense that we are at a meeting that will make a difference. A decisive moment has been reached. The decision about to be taken will have a significant impact. We are at a *kairos* moment, for *kairos* refers to a decisive or transforming or critical time.

While *chronos* must be used responsibly, leaders sense the *kairos* moments in life. As we use *chronos* time wisely, *kairos* moments occur. Most days pass by without having a *kairos* point. But *kairos* moments do open up in the course of *chronos*, and good leaders are alert to them. Indeed, the best leaders help to precipitate them.

Stephen Covey has developed a four-quadrant approach to the use of time. He looks at the intersection between those activities which are important and those which are not, and those which are urgent, and those which are not, suggesting that the meeting of each leads to four quadrants. Different kinds of activities can be fitted into each of the quadrants. Figure 10.1 is a slightly modified version of Covey's model.[2]

Urgent matters are usually visible. They press on us and scream for attention. We feel justified in dropping everything to get them attended to, because most often there is a negative short-term consequence if we do not. Sometimes they are fun. The phone that rings insists on being answered. The 'you've got mail' sign on your screen invites you to stop everything to check it. But so often what seems to be urgent turns out to be unimportant.

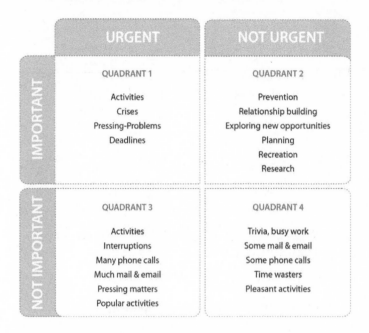

Figure 10.1: Time management matrix

Importance has to do with results. If something is important it contributes to your mission, values and high-priority goals.

We react to urgent matters. We have to be proactive about non-urgent ones. Quadrant 2 activities are usually the most important. Without them, we will have an endless stream of urgent fires to put out.

Quadrant 2 activities can include things like reading this book, or spending time with the family or developing new relationships. Doing important things before they are urgent often means that far more gets done and new strategic opportunities are created.

People often spend most of their time in one of the quadrants. The usual outcomes of this are shown in Figure 10.2.

The key then is to order our lives so that we spend most time working in Quadrant 2. We may have fewer adrenaline surges, but more will be accomplished.

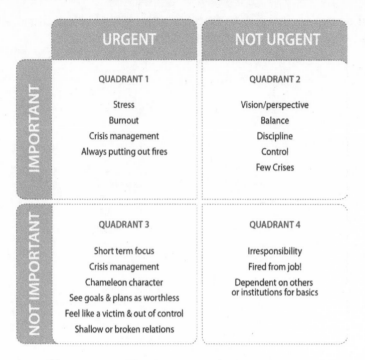

	URGENT	NOT URGENT
IMPORTANT	**QUADRANT 1** Stress Burnout Crisis management Always putting out fires	**QUADRANT 2** Vision/perspective Balance Discipline Control Few Crises
NOT IMPORTANT	**QUADRANT 3** Short term focus Crisis management Chameleon character See goals & plans as worthless Feel like a victim & out of control Shallow or broken relations	**QUADRANT 4** Irresponsibility Fired from job! Dependent on others or institutions for basics

Figure 10.2: Time management outcomes

A task

Think through your average week. Fill in the kinds of activities that fill each quadrant. Where does the bulk of your time and energy go? Explore ways you can enlarge the Quadrant 2 sector of your life.

Running effective meetings

Those in leadership often feel that their life is a non-stop series of meetings. Given the amount of time that leaders spend in meetings, it is often surprising that they don't spend more time ensuring that meetings are optimal, and not just time-wasters.

Imbibing some key guidelines can help. A 'top ten' check list follows. The leader in you will immediately relate this to your context to see if any changes are needed.

1. *Have a clear goal or goals* for the meeting. What is it that the meeting hopes to achieve? Too often meetings are 'because we have a meeting every week'. This is not necessarily wrong if the goal of the meeting is to ensure that lines of communication between people are kept open, especially if the meeting is structured in such a way as to ensure that each person leaves fully informed. In other words, the meeting should be designed to ensure meaningful communication happens if this is the goal of the meeting.

2. *Invite the right people* to the meeting. Too often meetings are attended by people who don't need to be there. Not only does this waste their time, but if the focus of the meeting is outside their area of expertise, they may lead the group into unhelpful detours – or simply become bored and prove distracting to others. Likewise, if those with the power to make the required decisions are not present, little is likely to be achieved by the discussion.

3. *Send out invitations to the meeting* with sufficient lead time to increase the likelihood of attendance. If the initial invites go out well in advance, it is a good idea to ensure that an email reminder is sent about a week beforehand.

4. *Circulate the agenda in advance.* Rather than simply circulating a list of agenda items, provide a sentence or two of background so that people know the key areas of concern and why the item is on the agenda. Sometimes it is appropriate to put a rough time allocation next to items so that people are alerted to the expected length of discussion for each agenda item – though as this can be controversial and is sometimes seen to be controlling, sensitivity is needed. Notify people of any updates to the agenda. If papers need to be read in advance, ensure that people have enough time to do so. At the start of the meeting agree on a priority list for the agenda. It is not always necessary to stick to the order in the agenda – especially if some key members have to leave before the end or it is clear that some items are especially complex and will require the group to think through the issue while they are still fresh.

5. *Set a definite start and end time to the meeting, and stick to it.* Alert the group to the progress of time at key points in the meeting. A chairman willing to say, 'We've been going for about an hour

now and are due to finish in another hour. We've only got to item two of eight, so can we make sure we don't repeat points', is valuable.

6. *Start promptly.* If you regularly wait for people to arrive, they will always be late. Set an 'on time' norm from the start. Remember, if there are six people at the meeting, and it starts ten minutes late, you have wasted an hour.

7. *Appoint the right chairperson.* This should be someone who can be pleasantly firm, ensuring that people stick to the task at hand, while being sufficiently experienced to realize that on occasion allowing a little longer on some items is wise.

8. *Make sure that a reliable person is assigned to take minutes.* Decisions should be clearly recorded, required actions crisply noted, people responsible for taking the actions recorded and the date by which the action is to be taken stated. Budget allocation can also be listed if appropriate. It is usually helpful to lay out minutes with a clear 'action by and when' column.

9. *If possible, complete and distribute minutes the day of the meeting.* Nowadays the minute-taker will usually have a minute template set up on their laptop to enable the first draft of the minutes to be very close to the final draft. Ideally they should get the chair to check the draft of the minutes immediately the meeting ends, make any required changes on the spot, and then email them to the group the same day. As technology improves, it is increasingly common for minutes to be projected up as they are taken during the meeting. Any inaccurate recording of decisions can then be rectified immediately.

10. *Obtain any updates on actions in advance of the next meeting.* These can be incorporated into the agenda for the next meeting. So, for example, in the 'matters arising from the last meeting' item, a comment can update on what has happened.

A task

Reread these ten guidelines, giving your organization a tick (or not) for those that are followed. What is the score? As a quiet leader, how can you work to get it to ten? Do you disagree with some of the points or would some be inappropriate in your setting? If so, why?

Delegation

A key leadership skill is delegation. Leaders who don't delegate quickly become swamped with small tasks that prevent them from their primary task of leading. The art of delegating is closely linked to two skills: the wise selection of who to delegate to followed by the appropriate balance between freedom and supervision.

1. Select who to delegate to. The acronym FAT is often cited. Look for people who are
   - Faithful (they turn up, and they do what they say they will do)
   - Available (they have the time to do the task; this needs to be balanced with the insight that if you want a task done, get a busy person to do it)
   - Trainable. This is the quiet leadership principle. We don't require people to be spectacular achievers before we delegate tasks to them, but we do require them to be willing to learn and to receive constructive feedback. Often the supervision and mentoring of trainable people can also be delegated.
2. Find the right balance between freedom and supervision. We should neither delegate and abandon nor delegate and micromanage. The particular mix adopted is impacted by the skill set and experience of the person to whom we have delegated the task. Usually people need some guidance at the start, and less as time goes by. Those who need too much supervision are not good choices to delegate tasks to as the time taken to monitor them erodes the value of having delegated the task. This must be balanced by a willingness to give beginners more time, as if the choice of person is sound the longer-term benefits will be great.

When delegating, we need to be clear about what task/s we are delegating, what the limit of the person's responsibility and authority is, the appropriate reporting line and who to appeal to if assistance is required or questions need to be answered, and the required timeframe. Over time quiet leaders get to know their team well enough to make good decisions concerning delegation. A common error is to regard someone as incapable because they did not perform as expected in the past. While past performance is often an indicator of future performance, if delegating did not work in the past, carefully evaluate why it did not work. Often the reason is that expectations were not clarified or that the task was not clearly explained. Sometimes it is that a task was only partly delegated, and the person became confused about what they were supposed to be doing.

The worst delegators are those who pretend to delegate but are inflexible perfectionists who believe there is only one way to do things. Inevitably the person they delegate the task to does not do it exactly their way, so they rush in and rescue the situation by doing the task themself, thereby proving (usually only to themself) that they are indispensible. They then feel justified in proclaiming that delegation never works and invariably takes more time than doing the task yourself.

To be a successful delegator, be clear about what the final outcome should be, and then watch in delight at the creative and different routes people take to get there. This does not mean that some guidance should not be given along the way, but it pays to remember that most people hate it when others constantly look over their shoulder. We should make it clear that we (or, if you are a really good delegator, another suitable person) are available to discuss the project further and to provide assistance when needed. For larger tasks, request progress reports. Though most people are both creative and responsible, some will never admit to being out of their depth. Systematically charting progress can help ensure that projects stay on track.

In deciding to whom to delegate a task, identify those for whom it will be a doable stretch. People respond best to things that are a bit of a challenge, so long as it is attainable. Bill Hybels helpfully distinguishes between 'doable hard versus destructive hard'.[3] Doable hard is when we put ourselves out, learn new things, take time and effort, but in the end feel that it was worthwhile because we achieved something of value. Doable hard is when something was difficult, but the reward from it was such that we are perfectly willing to do it again. Destructive hard is when we are so out of our depth that it is clear we will never make it to the shore without some serious losses. We are left feeling depleted and have little to show for it. At times we might succeed, but at so high a cost that we are not willing to venture out again. In doing so we win the battle, but lose the war.

There are exceptions to the doable hard guideline. If the organization is under a great deal of pressure or people are generally overwhelmed by the complexity they face it may be wiser to delegate the task to someone who can do it in autopilot. For all that, remember that when life is filled only with the routine, we stop growing and lose our edge. Quiet leaders help to ensure that those on their team continue to grow by facing enough doable hard challenges.

To ponder

Rate your delegation skills. What areas do you need to work on? If you don't believe that delegation is worthwhile ('I always land up having to do it myself!') challenge your excuses. Can you delegate differently to ensure a better outcome?

Conflict resolution

While we would like to believe that people united behind a common mission and vision will automatically work together harmoniously, reality is often a little different. The Bible teaches that all people are made in the image of God, but as a result of the fall our lives are lived well short of this lofty status. Nowhere is the impact of the fall more obvious than in the realm of interpersonal relationships. Even in the best organizations there is often conflict between team members. Sometimes it is overt, at other times it is masked behind factual but uncharitable statements about others.

Many of us find ourselves confused in conflict situations. We often interpret things through our own grid of insecurity, reading nuances into statements when none were intended. This is particularly true in team situations where we are working closely with people who have the same heart for God but have different priorities and agendas. It can be confusing to find yourself at loggerheads with someone you rather like.

Justin Dennison suggests that to understand a conflict situation, we should define whom the conflict is between and what the conflict is about.[4] He expands on this by differentiating between a few spheres:

Who is the conflict between?

Intra-personal conflict: This is conflict within an individual which could be a result of insecurity, low self-worth or feeling insignificant. No one outside can resolve a conflict emanating from within a person, though we can help people to face unresolved personal issues, and work to create an environment of hopefulness which gives people the courage to face hard personal questions. If we normalize the need for personal growth and development and value self-awareness in people, we make it easier for them to embark on a journey of personal change. It might not be immediately obvious that the conflict is an intra-personal one, in that the inner turmoil inside of the person might see them lash out at others. On the surface it might therefore seem to be an interpersonal conflict. The clue is usually given when you discover the same person involved in conflict over and over again. Where this is the case it is usually safe to assume that this has less to do with the people who are being accused and is more about the unresolved issues inside of the individual.

Inter-personal conflict: Here the conflict is between individuals. It often has very little to do with the group's mission, and may have resulted from a clash of personalities, a misunderstanding, jealousy . . . indeed, any of the many reasons that cause people to belittle and dislike each other.

Intra-group conflict: Here the conflict is between groups within a team. Sometimes strengths and weaknesses are closely aligned. Some team leaders are very effective at creating a sense of togetherness and belonging within their group. Clearly this is a good thing. At times, however, group cohesion is gained by belittling the achievements of other groups within the team. This is less than helpful, and works off the myth that if some other group does something poorly, it proves that we must be doing it well . . . flawed logic at the best of times. For example, in an educational setting the administrative staff might cohere together wonderfully, but unite in viewing the teaching staff as overpaid and underworked. Or the maintenance staff might view the IT staff as indulged and impractical. Sometimes the division might cross work categories. Those who have been on the staff for longer might form a little clique that is closed to more recent recruits. They might systematically block any suggestions coming from those who are newer because they have not yet proved their worth to the organization, and so it goes on. A key Christian virtue is hospitality, which involves more than providing food and shelter for another. It involves being genuinely open to the other and a willingness to value the world of the other. It frees the other to be different from me while still being fully respected.

Inter-group conflict: Here the conflict is between different groups or teams. It is conflict on a slightly wider scale, though sometimes it is less personal as a result. It could be that a primary and secondary school on the same site lapse into conflict. Primary staff might feel obligated to be disparaging about senior school staff and vice versa. Or it could be that the local Presbyterian church feels obligated to be insulting about its Pentecostal neighbour. The tragedy of such conflicts is that usually the groups have comparable missions, even though they might set about achieving them slightly differently.

What is the conflict about?

We should not only clarify who the conflict is between but also what the conflict is over. Surprisingly often people leave this in the realm of the vague. If we don't know just what people are clashing over, the likelihood of solving the actual problem is slight. Some conflicts have a substantive basis, usually based on something that has happened. Others are more attitudinal, and stem from tone, nuance or perceived insult.

Substantive conflict: Here the conflict might be about facts, values and traditions, methods and means, ends and goals. Through open discussion the issues should clarify and can often be resolved. Substantive conflicts usually provide you something tangible to work with. It could be 'We were not given a fair share of the profits from the fundraiser' or 'Our team members were not acknowledged when everyone else was thanked' or 'You chose to hold that event on a Sunday knowing that clashed with the religious convictions of most members in our group'.

Attitudinal conflict: This can be a little more difficult to define accurately, but is about feelings, perspectives and possibly prejudices. No matter how successfully you resolve conflict over a particular issue, the conflict will recur on other issues if the role of attitudes is not acknowledged and dealt with. For example, a substantive conflict might be 'We were not given a fair share of the profits from the fundraiser' which might be resolved after open discussion. However, if the attitude that led to the conflict was that one group felt empowered to proclaim the division of profits from the event without due consultation, that same attitude is likely to see another substantive conflict birthed in the future. The example is a good one in that many conflicts are masked power struggles – one group or individual trying to assert their right to tell another what to do. Even if the decisions they make are benevolent, the underlying attitude 'We have the power to proclaim, you do not' will cause repeated conflicts.

Most of us don't like conflict and hope it will somehow solve itself. We would rather look the other way and pretend we did not see or hear anything. We would rather sweep it under the carpet and hope no one notices. Yet it will not go away. Time does not heal conflict, only resolution can do that. Conflict can be messy, tiresome, exhausting and embarrassing. We might repeatedly replay difficult conversations in our head or toss and turn sleeplessly at night. It is emotionally, psychologically, physically and spiritually draining. Yet people are people. Those committed to achieving tasks in the close confines of a team will sometimes experience conflict. If worked through constructively, conflict can be a sign of the gospel, which is about reconciliation – indeed, reconciliation achieved through no less a price than the cross of Christ.

Conflict is much less likely to occur where trust has been built up over time. Where there is trust, the default drive of team members is to assume the most charitable explanation when things go wrong. Where trust is missing, the default veers towards suspicion. At times it plunges towards paranoia. Consequently quiet leaders invest time in building trust.

Trust grows when people find you have stuck to your word and been consistent over the long haul. Each time we are consistent and dependable, trust grows. Each time we aren't, trust erodes.

Here are some key principles for building trust:

1. Do what you say you will do. One of the reasons the Bible urges us to be slow to make promises is that, once made, they must be kept. Don't promise what you can't do. If you have made a promise you can't keep, front up and be open and transparent about it.
2. Be there. Turning up regularly builds confidence.
3. Pay what you owe when it is due. If you can't, speak to the relevant people and work out a plan.
4. Act honourably even in the face of temptation or criticism. Don't slander others when they aren't present (or when they are). People will assume you'll do the same to them when they are absent – and they are probably right. Acting honourably when unfairly maligned helps win the trust and loyalty of people. If under pressure you hold to your key convictions and remain a servant leader, they will trust you to treat them similarly when you see things in a different light.
5. Tell the truth about yourself and others. Work at portraying others in a good light. Remember the Pauline principle that the truth is always to be spoken in love.[5] If we are deeply resentful about someone it is often best to refrain from speaking about them until our attitude towards them starts to change. It requires us to check our internal motivation in embarking upon a conversation. Before we say something critical about another, we should ask if what we are about to say is both truthful and if it needs to be said.
6. Acknowledge mistakes. Transparency is very powerful. If we are willing to talk about our own weaknesses and flaws, other people will not need to.
7. Be a servant leader and put the welfare of others first.
8. Learn to disagree without drawing blood. Quiet leaders think carefully about the language they use. In tense situations they learn to speak without exclamation marks. As a rule of thumb, exaggeration is a wonderful gift when telling a humorous story at a dinner party, but understatement works far better in conflict. It is worth replaying conversations to check if we could have said things more kindly. If we do this often enough, charitable conversation will come naturally to us. This will birth

enormous dividends over time. I am not suggesting that we should not be frank and honest. However the truth is usually heard more clearly when it is spoken quietly and calmly.

No one is completely versatile in managing conflict. Some will go to great lengths to avoid conflict. Others are glad to meet it head-on, using their authority to force submission. Some prefer to listen to those who have grievances and others try to point out where they're wrong.

Leas suggests that there are six distinct personal conflict management styles.[6] He notes that our conflict style might be different in different settings. For example, at work we might be primarily persuading and collaborating, while at home with our teenagers we might oscillate between negotiating and bargaining and avoiding or accommodating. Each style is appropriate in some settings and is summarized below with a description of situations in which it may be appropriate.

1. *Persuading*: This is the most frequently used of all the strategies. It involves attempting to persuade others using rational approaches and arguments in an attempt to convince them that you are right and that they need to change. This strategy assumes that the other person is incorrect or ignorant and needs to change. Persuasion strategies are useful when conflict is at a low level and the other person recognizes your expertise or trusts your ideas. Persuasion strategies seldom work if there is serious conflict, especially when trust is low.

2. *Compelling or forcing*: Compelling is the use of physical or emotional force, authority or pressure to oblige or constrain someone to do (not think) what you want. Most compelling comes through the use of authority (the right we give to a person or group to make decisions for us). All organizations have a contract (explicit or tacit) that indicates authority. While compelling may be important in an emergency, if compelling strategies are used consistently, relationships deteriorate, manipulation emerges, rebellion simmers, and abuse is rife.

3. *Avoiding, ignoring, accommodating or fleeing*: Here conflict is avoided by staying away from it or by pretending it doesn't

exist. Those who adopt this style flee conflict by removing themself from the place where conflict may occur. They accommodate conflict by going along with the *opposition* and putting harmonious relationships before dealing with the issue. Common avoidance strategies include procrastination, not doing what was promised, ignoring the issues, pretending to support something while in fact being part of the problem, or studying the problem with no intention of doing anything. Sometimes conflict is best ignored or accommodated, for example, when attempts to deal with the conflict are likely to escalate it or when the other party does not have the emotional resources to work through the conflict, or when the difference is minor and of little consequence. But when conflict is ignored it tends to escalate. As people can grow from loving confrontation, we remove an opportunity for growth by ignoring the conflict.

4. *Collaborating*: Those with a collaborative conflict resolution strategy try to involve all concerned in finding a solution. The problem is tackled together. It involves jointly acknowledging and defining the problem, agreeing on the process of dealing with the problem, looking for options that offer mutual gains, and making a cooperative decision. Collaboration only really works when there is trust between those in conflict. All information must be shared. This does not happen in a low-trust environment. Collaborative strategies are desirable because all parties then have a strong commitment to the outcome.

5. *Negotiating or bargaining*: In negotiation the expectations are lower than in collaboration. People know that they're not going to get everything they want, but are willing to give some ground in order to find a solution. Negotiation is a 'some-win, some-lose' strategy. You make initial demands that you know won't be met. You argue for *your* case, but are willing to accept that some elements of the opposition's case will be acceptable. In negotiating people only share what is helpful to their case. Negotiation can be used at all levels of conflict if the desired outcomes are not mutually exclusive. Success is more likely if the parties have comparable power.

6. *Supporting*: The major assumption of support strategies is that the other person is the one with the problem and therefore you

don't have to deal with the problem, but can support them as they deal with the issue. You are not trying to fix the problem, but will help them as they deal with their difficulties. If you warn, judge, correct, compel or bargain with the person, you are stepping outside your support role. This strategy is best when you are not involved in the conflict or when you don't believe the tension is motivated by the issue at hand.

A leadership interview with Bridget Aitchison

Dr Bridget Aitchison is the vice-president for the college of adult and professional studies at Indiana Wesleyan University. She has an exceptional record of institutional leadership.

1. Bridget, as a vice-president of a large university with a global presence, time must always feel like it is in short supply. Do you long for a 25-hour day, or have you mastered some time management skills that readers might find helpful?
I think I actually need a 30-hour day! By nature, I am a workaholic. I am one of those people who only needs four to five hours of sleep a night as long as it is unbroken sleep. That said, work/life balance is very important no matter what your energy or capacity is. I have a few things I do to keep that balance – I start every day reading the word of God and praying. I ask God, 'What do *you* want me to do today?' and then I spend time listening. I try to end each day this way too. I also try to take one day a month where I am 'off the reservation'. No one knows where I am, my phone is off, and I don't look at emails if I don't want to. It's a day to strategize, think about the bigger-picture issues, do the higher-level thinking and spend time with the Lord and recharge. It's important to have a way to get out of the weeds on a regular basis and gain perspective. I make it a point to laugh more than I worry. Once every three to four months I try to take a long weekend to do 'anything'. This is a 'no responsibility' weekend. I don't have to clean the house, do dishes, and answer emails or write reports if I don't want to. I can stay home and read all day, or I can get away and sightsee, or play with my kids . . . pretty much anything I want that is fun and refreshes me within moral and legal limits. I make time for my

family. As a widow and mother, God's order is that my family come *before* my job. I have to remind myself of that, especially now that they are young adults and don't *seem* to need me as much. Once a year, I go on vacation for two weeks. In a row. It takes five to six days to actually unwind and let go of work so I need fourteen days in a row to really get totally rested and refreshed. The years I have not done this, I have come dangerously close to burn-out. Usually I break it down into a couple days at home, a week to ten days away on a real vacation, then a few more days at home for a stay-vacation. The other important thing is to not let email overwhelm you. I am an email junkie. My iphone is always with me. I'm learning to be the master of it so it does not master me. If you are checking your email every few minutes, you are not getting your work done. This one is hard for me but I'm working on it!

2. What advice would you give to readers who feel that their lives are consumed by meetings?
We have a meeting culture here at IWU. I can attend five to eight meetings on a regular workday. My philosophy is that a short meeting is a good meeting. If you can't get through the meeting in ninety minutes to two hours you aren't yet ready for the meeting to happen. Enough groundwork should be done beforehand that the meeting is about decision-making rather than overly focused on discussion. A good meeting chair has to keep the group on point. Don't go down the rabbit trails. Don't run around in circles. Be respectful of people's time. My first year here, I regularly chaired meetings that historically were scheduled for three to four hours. When did I get my work done? Nights and weekends. That is not sustainable. Now meetings are ninety minutes to two hours long. The expectation is that the preparation work is actually done before the meeting. If you are attending too many meetings, then start with the ones that you chair – ask yourself:

- Is this meeting really necessary?
- Can the decisions be reached or the information disseminated another way?
- How much time do we spend catching up on non-work things or discussing tangential information?

- How can I prevent that from happening and keep everyone on task?

If you are required to attend meetings chaired by others and don't have the authority to structure them, start talking to the other leaders. They may feel just as overwhelmed as you (in fact, they likely are!). See if there can be a consensus about length and frequency of meetings. Be an influence for change where you can.

3. How do you decide what to delegate and what to hold on to for yourself?
This one is always difficult. If you look at writings by John Maxwell and Jim Collins, they talk about five levels of leadership. One of the higher levels of leadership is marked by a leader who invests in the development of their employees. Part of this is to hire the right people for the right job (Collins' analogy is to put employees on the right seat in the bus) and let them do their job. It is important to know what is going on but not micro-manage it. Empower those who work for you to make decisions within certain parameters. Set the boundaries but then let them be creative. The work you should be doing are those things that fall within your skill set and strengths and that keep the whole train moving forward – work that is strategic by nature, big-picture view, and within your area of expertise. Otherwise, you will have hopefully hired people that are better than you in the area you have hired them for and you will delegate that work to them.

4. Christian organizations are supposed to be conflict-free, but it isn't really like that! How do you maintain your stance as a Christ follower in the midst of conflict-filled scenarios?
I tend to be a right-brained, creative, emotional person but I also switch to left-brained logical thinking. My early days in leadership were spent trying to figure out which one to act out of when. I didn't always get it right! In a conflict situation, it is better to not act emotionally. Christ encountered all sorts of conflict-filled scenarios in his lifetime (think of the money-changers whose booths he overturned in the temple courtyard). I try to judge the situation – when does it need me to step in and lay down how it is going to be, much like a parent? When is it better to mediate – giving each party a

chance to speak their piece then helping move them to an understanding of each other's positions and finally, hopefully, to a resolution that both can live with? When is it better to stay out of the situation all together? These questions have to be asked each time conflict arises and the answer will be different each time.

My first 'go to' in these situations is prayer. I ask God, 'Show me this situation through your wisdom and not my own limited knowledge'. Don't take sides immediately (even though you may have to eventually). Try to understand each person's point of view before you get involved. These are all guidelines that can help but I have one word of caution . . . as Christians we tend to often extend 'grace' in conflict situations. Often this amounts to nothing more than sweeping it under the rug and not actually dealing with it. Grace given too often and/or for the wrong reasons is detrimental to people's growth. It does not help in the long run to ignore, avoid or wholesale forgive without a process that leads to genuine resolution.

I remember a student in my early days of academic administration. She almost never handed in assignments on time nor did she get necessary paperwork in on time. She was always given extensions without accountability, or extended 'grace' when she missed deadlines. She learned that there was always a way to appeal and her appeals were always granted. As a result, she never made an effort to meet the deadlines. The 'grace' overextended exacerbated her behaviour. Once someone finally said, 'No', and stuck to it, she began to learn her lesson. After three immutable 'No's', she changed her behaviour. Because she had to suffer consequences and accountability, she changed her behaviour.

Overextending grace is one of the common downfalls of Christian organizations. It does more harm than good. Leaders should always be asking, what did Jesus model for us? How would he treat this situation? I'm sure there is a book in the making to answer those two questions!

5. Please pass on one key leadership insight you have.
Keep your priorities in order and your work/life balance sane. For me my priorities are God, family, work. The most important thing for me is to always keep God at the centre of who you are. The most important tool you have as a leader is your relationship

with God. Do whatever you need to do to continually strengthen and grow that relationship. 'But seek first his kingdom and his righteousness, and all these things will be given to you as well.'

For reflection

When next you find yourself in a conflict situation, think through the six approaches Leas outlines – persuading, compelling, avoiding, collaborating, negotiating and supporting. Do you think any of these strategies are particularly appropriate in your context? Are there any that should be avoided? Which come most naturally to you? Are there any you would never use and, if so, why?

11

Some Tortoise Triumphs:
Quiet Leadership in Practice

The key question for most people will always be, 'But does quiet leadership work in practice?' Although Jesus announces that the meek will inherit the earth, that day could be a long way off. Until then many will assume that while 'the tortoise usually wins' is a quaintly pleasing idea, in practice it is the exception rather than the rule.

As I pondered the question, I again realized that I have no gripe against hare-like leaders who are naturally gifted and for whom leadership comes easily. After all, effective leadership is in relatively short supply – so why oppose any form of leadership that empowers others and helps them to achieve what they otherwise would not have? The heartbeat of this book is that successful leadership is also within the reach of reluctant leaders and that it is attainable for those who are not so obviously located at the front of the pack. What evidence is there to back this thesis?

I live in the stunningly beautiful city of Perth in Western Australia. With a population of 1.8 million people it is Australia's fourth largest city, a long way behind both Sydney and Melbourne and trailing a fair way after Brisbane. Its location on the west coast of Australia leaves it far removed from the rest of the country and able to claim the title as the second most remote city in the world, only narrowly beaten by Auckland.[1]

When you live in a country's fourth largest city you meet many quiet leaders. After all, if you assume that bigger must be better you wouldn't choose to reside in Perth. The headquarters of most large Australian companies are in Sydney or Melbourne, so those who rise to the very top of Australian society tend to gravitate there. But as any Perth resident will tell you, you shouldn't be fooled by appearances. They will quickly remind you that when the global financial crisis struck, Australia was largely spared from its impact because of the buoyant economy of Western Australia. It just so happens that mining is Western Australia's key industry and, in spite of an otherwise stagnant world economy, the mineral boom has continued with barely a pause for a hare-like breather. In short, having stuck to its knitting (which happens to be mining) and having stuck to it tenaciously in good seasons and poor, Perth and Western Australia have found themselves as the unlikely but actual saviour of the Australian economy. The tortoise wins!

It has not just been in economic matters that Perth has surprised. Excuse me if I sound a little parochial as I cite local examples, but I do want to earth this work in reality, and I hope that the following two case-studies will provide you with hope and inspiration for your setting – wherever it happens to be. Naturally I am telling the story with the permission of the people involved.

So why have the Baptist churches of Western Australia grown so much faster than elsewhere?

As is the case in most Western countries, the Christian church has experienced slow but steady decline in Australia. In rounded figures, in the 2006 Australian census 64 per cent of Australians affirmed some kind of allegiance to the Christian faith. By the 2011 census the figure had declined to 61 per cent. This follows on from significant declines from previous census results making the overall trend unmistakable and disturbing. A closer analysis of the census data unveils the fortunes of individual denominations. Some have fared better than others. Baptists are one of the few denominations that have managed to grow faster than the population growth rate, growing by 11.3 per cent during the census period, a time in which the Australian population grew by 8.3 per cent, making for overall growth of 3 per cent in real terms. A deeper dig into the statistics reveals that a large part of this growth can be attributed to the growth of Baptists in the state of Western Australia, where during the five-year census period they grew by 27.3 per cent, 13 per cent ahead of the state's overall growth of 14.3 per cent. So why have Baptist churches in Western Australia grown so much faster than elsewhere?

The story begins with the 2001 appointment of Steve Smith to the post of Director of Ministries for the Baptist Union of Western Australia. Steve would be the first to say that he is a reluctant leader. Indeed he would claim that his appointment filled him with a genuine sense of fear, even terror. It was not unjustified. Most of the denominational indicators were poor. Structures were clumsy and dysfunctional, the churches had been through some bitter theological controversies and were generally trapped in a mindset which had been unhelpful in the twentieth century, and was likely to be disastrous in the twenty-first. Though some new churches had been planted, they were usually a product of a church split. Rather than being stories of hope and inspiration, too often their founding narrative was one of disgruntlement, intolerance and suspicion. There were some alternate stories that could be told, stories where churches had found innovative and creative ways to link with their community. Some schools had been started, one church built and housed itself in a basketball centre, yet others had started to dream of ways to connect more effectively with their community. Sadly, the exceptions only proved the rule.

Steve quickly realized that the denomination faced a fundamental choice, summed up by a visiting consultant as selecting between a slow painful death and painful but transforming change. Not assuming that people would prefer the latter, Steve embarked on a series of consultations. One talkfest followed another. It involved tortoise-like plodding, many one-on-one conversations, repeating the same argument over and over again, but eventually the churches voted for meaningful change.

To state the obvious, if things are to change they cannot remain the same. It was acknowledged that a new era would require a new constitution. This constitution was designed to empower dreams. The focus of many constitutions is on ensuring that nothing ever goes wrong. While a noble goal, in practice such constitutions are usually equally effective in ensuring that nothing ever goes right. Indeed, the previous constitution had made it very difficult for anything to ever happen. However a changed constitution alone would never be enough. There needed to be a shift in attitude and a fresh vision of what was possible.

As people spoke of their hopes and dreams for the future, several themes emerged. People longed for a day when churches would cease to be ghettoes of escape but rather centres of mission and empowerment. The sentiment was captured when someone suggested that we shift from being inwardly to outwardly tilted. It was recommended that every church programme be scrutinized with the question, 'How does this benefit the people we are trying to impact?' rather than 'How does this benefit us?' It represented a significant change of tune. Churches realized that much of their energy was going into hosting programmes that were of little or no relevance to the community they were trying to reach.

They also discovered that they had regularly erred in engaging in vigorous debate over issues that at best would draw a bored 'whatever' from the constituency they were called to serve. The 1980s had seen a bitter and unseemly war over whether we should classify the Bible as an inerrant text, or as our supreme authority, or as a text that is entirely trustworthy. Interesting though this debate is, it had become increasingly clear that the community outside the four walls of the church found it of negligible interest, and were perplexed by the acrimonious tone of the discussion. Their preference was for a different song. Actually it was not only those outside the church who desired an alternate tune; those inside its walls were increasingly searching for a way out, as became clear with the rise of what New Zealand sociologist Alan Jamieson has called 'churchless faith'.[2] In short, even Christians couldn't stomach the fare being served at the average local church.

Change never occurs automatically, and usually some key people have to be put in place to ensure it is nudged along. Steve Smith recommended that we appoint a church health consultant – someone who had pastoral credibility and who would get alongside churches to help them to review what they were doing and to assess if it was likely to result in their achieving their aspirations. If not, the consultant would help the church devise a different strategy. Phil Bryant was appointed to the position. This required a step of faith by the denomination, as there was no obvious way to fund the post.

A word about money is in place here. Charismatic leaders are usually confident of their ability to raise funds. They are typically

178

bold and their dynamism is often enough to persuade people to part with their money and entrust it to the cause championed by the leader. Quiet leaders are often at a significant disadvantage here, but need to operate from a settled disposition that money follows vision, and that if they guide a group in the right direction, and are open, transparent and accountable about money, there will be enough. This is the stance that the Baptist Union of Western Australia decided to adopt and, in spite of limited funds, they refused to be governed by what was termed 'a poverty mentality'. Rather than ask, 'Can we afford this?' it was agreed to ask, 'Do we believe that this should be done?' We decided to operate from the premise that if we really believed that something should be done, money would become available to make it possible.

At the start it involved a willingness to risk the small reserves that had been built over a hundred-year period. Many of these reserves were designated for purposes that were no longer relevant. The BUWA's business manager, Terry Hicks, had to work hard to get these restrictions removed. In practice, it has not been necessary to touch these reserves. Indeed, even in post-inflationary terms they have swelled significantly since the decision was made to do what we needed to do, rather than what we felt we could afford to do. This highlights that money is never really the issue, but that a sense of call and commitment to a worthy vision is.

If the churches were to be guided towards health, it was decided that our key training institution should partner with the denomination in the process of change. The Baptist Theological College of Western Australia had built a reputation for academic excellence, but its reputation for pastoral relevance was a little less enviable. It was recognized that this deficiency needed to be addressed. The imminent retirement of some of the staff of the college allowed the denomination to dream of an alternate future. It decided to appoint what it termed a 'leader for change' and instructed the new principal to use that title in the opening years of his tenure. As I was the one appointed to this post, I know the subsequent chapters rather well!

I classify myself as a quiet leader, and found the task of transforming the college easier than was generally anticipated. First, things are rarely as bad as people try to suggest, so I discovered more residual strength and goodwill in the college than might have been expected. The previous principal went out of his way to ensure the success of my tenure. Though retired, he continues to play a meaningful role. Second, I was appointed with the express mandate to introduce change, so people would have been disappointed if nothing had happened. There was an openness to change that I had not masterminded, but it made my task considerably easier.

Step 1 was to win back the trust of the churches. Once we could assign that to the 'largely achieved' basket, we needed to listen closely to what the churches were saying. We realized that the college was being criticized for doing what it could never do, namely, it was not producing graduates who the day after graduation would be ready to provide wise and flawless leadership to even the most problematic of local churches – and usually only the most problematic churches were sufficiently desperate to employ recent graduates. While the critique was unfair and unrealistic, beneath the flawed complaint there was a valid concern. It was clear that ongoing professional development for pastors was required.

We decided to birth a leadership centre to supplement (but never replace) the work of the theological college. While we were making this change, it seemed an appropriate time for a new name, so instead of being the Baptist Theological College of Western Australia we became Vose Seminary, a seminary which today houses several centres of excellence, the first of which was Vose Leadership. In less than a decade our numbers have quintupled, and we are in the process of forming a new college of higher education which will offer courses in addition to theology. This flows from our conviction that theology is not only relevant for the church, but also for the marketplace. The Christ story should make a decisive difference to the way in which we approach economics, education, the social sciences . . . the list goes on and on. This journey has just begun. It will be lovely to discuss the outcomes in a decade or two – by which time we hope that Vose College of Higher Education will have become Vose University. It has been a one-step-at-a-time journey. We overestimate what can be achieved in a year, but underestimate what can be done in a decade, provided we stay on course.

Has the growth of the seminary contributed to the rapid growth of the denomination? Undoubtedly. It is not the only reason but it has added to the relevance of a denomination willing to challenge its excuses and to ask the probing question, 'How does this benefit the people we are trying to impact?' as opposed to 'How does this benefit us?'

Steve Smith completed his term as Director of Ministries at the end of 2006. His initial five-year term had been extended by a year, after which both he and the denomination agreed that while he had been the ideal person to lead the denomination through a period of dramatic change, he was not the person to capitalize on the growth that would result from the change. It is here that reluctant leaders are at a great advantage. Steve didn't want to cling onto the leadership – indeed he never really wanted to be the leader at all. He had accepted that in the overall journey of transformation for the Baptist Union of Western Australia, he was the one called to initiate change. Though he did so with fear and trepidation, he was persistent and tenacious. He rose above his anxieties, involved others in the process of change, and kept putting one foot in front of the next. After six years he knew it was time for a more colourful leader to cement and build upon the foundations laid. Quiet leaders know the right time to leave. He left when the changes he had implemented were so strong it was unlikely they would be undone. The tortoise won . . .

A word about the motivation of quiet leaders is in order. Reluctant leaders take up the mantle of leadership because they realize that, reluctant though they might be, something needs to happen. I am reminded of a newspaper account I read where a woman suffering from hydrophobia was asked how she overcame her fear of water to leap into a flooded river to rescue her 3-year-old nephew. She recounted that as she stood on the riverbank paralysed by fear, she was suddenly overcome with a greater fear, the fear of doing nothing . . . Quiet leaders identify with that story. They often come to leadership because doing nothing is the more frightening option. Though Steve never sought for the overall leadership of the Baptist Union of Western Australia, the option of doing nothing in the face of need was one he could not seriously contemplate. So he stepped up to the mark and made a difference.

Steve's successor, Mark Wilson, is a charismatic leader. He has been able to leverage the changes made during Steve's tenure for optimal impact. The movement has professionalized and adjusted to many of the challenges it faces as Australia continues to drift towards a hardened form of secularism. The fruit is there for everyone to see. The denomination has grown 13 per cent faster than the population over a five-year period. The impact of a quiet leader followed by a naturally charismatic leader has been considerable. I have said repeatedly that I am not opposed to heroic leaders. Their gifting is such that they will always make a contribution. My sadness is that quiet leaders often don't step up to the plate as they doubt that they can make a difference. In this actual-life scenario, a quiet leader followed by a charismatic leader has proved to be remarkably effective and has achieved results most would have thought impossible in the current climate.

The Carey story

Walk onto the Carey campus and you step onto a thriving campus that houses a college of 1,300 pupils, a bustling childcare centre, a growing church, and an ever-expanding range of community projects. Around 200 people are employed by the Carey movement, and that number is soon likely to double as an additional site has been purchased on which to duplicate everything being done at the founding site. In addition a large community centre is about to be built. The plans are outlined in a document entitled 'Carey 2014', a visionary document penned in 2009 after extensive consultation with the Carey constituency. It outlines what the Carey group hopes to achieve between 2009 and 2014 and, writing as I do in 2012, I can confirm that the vision is remarkably on target.

If you met the youthful crew who started Carey in the 1990s, you'd realize that the safe money would have bet on their failing in their ambition to start a church and a school. The group's logic was simple. Most Australians are not looking for a church to attend, and churches which assume that they are experience rapid decline. They decided to plant a church that would be 'turned inside out' – to quote the mantra they adopted. Instead of expecting the community to make their way to the church, they would ensure that the church was incarnated in the community in such a way that residents in the area could not help but bump into it over and over again. They decided to plant a school and, via providing outstanding education, they hoped to win the right to speak to the community about the deeper matters of life. Broadly stated the strategy was to build missional platforms, each platform providing a service of undisputed excellence, and via establishing credibility through excellent service provision, to utilize the opportunities which arose from the inevitable question, 'Why do you do this?' to point to the reality of Jesus and his love and compassion for all. In short, the vision has been to build and cross missional platforms – directing people to Jesus in the process.

The decision to start by planting a school has proved sound. The land the small group purchased was in a relatively deserted area and, while demographic studies suggested that the area would be developed in due course, no one can ever be certain how many years will pass before proposed developments eventuate. While they were building a school, they desperately prayed that there would be pupils to fill it. Their prayers were answered with seventy-three pupils enrolling for the first year – a number which has grown every year since.

An advantage of linking a school and a church together is the long association that families have with a school. As Carey offers pre-primary, primary and secondary schooling, families with several children sometimes have a twenty-year journey with the college. It provides a lot of time to make a difference in the life of a family. Given that the church is at the heart of all that the school does, families cannot but meet representatives from the church. Over the years, many of these encounters have proved to be transforming.

So who were the unlikely leaders who birthed the Carey movement? They were a group of about twenty-five twenty-somethings, heavily mortgaged, sometimes with young children, sometimes not having reached that stage. Though a fairly gifted group, they had little experience. They were led by a young pastor, Steve Izett. He believed that God had called this group to birth Carey and that, because God had called them, it could be done. He was willing to dream, and to speak of his dreams as though they would come true. In some ways Steve is not a quiet leader. His ability to cast vision is exceptional, and it comes naturally to him. In that sense he is a charismatic leader. However, Steve would be the first to list his many leadership flaws. He has succeeded because of the loyal band of followers who were willing to cover for those flaws.

The role of followers in the success of any movement is significant. It is often said that if you want to know if you are a leader, look behind you. If no one is in sight, you can't be a leader, because a leader without followers is a contradiction in terms. While this is true, it can underestimate the difference that followers can make, especially those who are willing to help lead from the second, third or fourth chair. While Steve was undoubtedly the overall leader of the group that founded Carey, the strength of his leadership was demonstrated via his openness to have others guide from behind. Steve tends to pay little attention to detail; others in the group did. Steve struggles to express his ideas in writing; others in the group filled that role. Steve sometimes forgets to follow up on key contacts; others in the group would nudge him into making the call, or make it if he was distracted. Steve can become discouraged; others in the group helped to ensure that no one lost heart. I could carry on, but the point is simple. Quiet leaders ensure that all bases get covered; they do not have to cover each base themself. Followers willing to fill the gaps left by a leader are instrumental in ensuring the overall success of any enterprise. They can only do this if the leader is wise enough to leave space for them to operate. Steve proved that he possessed such wisdom. If the leader is quickly defensive ('What gaps?'), the leader is left to juggle all the balls in the air, and invariably they start to fall.

Many leaders are fortunate to have a quiet leader alongside, helping to lead from the second chair. Steve had such a person in David Kilpatrick, who has served as the chair of the board since the start of the movement. A lawyer by profession, Dave has persistently helped Carey stay on target. He has been willing to ask the hard questions, while never losing hope and vision.

Around 2006 Carey started to lose direction. The school was well established, but the church was floundering. A commitment to build a community centre had come to nothing. Efforts to find land to start another campus had produced no viable leads. In spite of having contact with over a thousand families, relatively few were connecting with the church. The youth group was small – surprising given that the church had contact with hundreds of teenagers at the college. There was the danger that having spent so much energy building a missional platform, few would cross it.

A word about the cost of leadership is in order here. Steve Izett had provided outstanding visionary leadership to Carey for over a decade. It had come with a significant personal price tag. Truth to tell, Steve was close to burn-out. Even in successful movements, lots of things go wrong. Carey was no exception. Some staff appointments did not turn out as expected. Some relationships soured. There were some disappointments. Leadership can be lonely at such times.

In addition, the pioneer of a movement is not always the right person to take it on to maturity. In the early stages of a movement, when there is little to lose, a leader who is willing to take risks is highly valued. Once the group is established and has much to lose, a slightly more cautious approach is often called for.

In what was simultaneously a painful but very mature move, Steve decided to step down from his post as senior pastor of Carey at the end of 2008. He accepted an alternate post at Carey for three years before embracing a new challenge to cast vision for a depleted church in South Perth. It was a post which required a pioneer, willing to take risks to birth something new. He was sent into his new post knowing that he had the full support of the Carey community. The early signs are very encouraging.

My story overlaps with the Carey story in that after Steve stepped down as senior pastor, I was asked to take on the role while remaining in my position as principal of Vose Seminary. I have always been keen for all staff at the seminary to have a close connection with a local church to ensure that the training we provide for future church leaders is rooted in the reality of actual church life. While intrigued by the possibility of simultaneously serving at Carey and Vose, I wondered if it would be possible. My meetings with the key players at Carey convinced me that it would be a viable option. Vose already operated with a strong leadership team, and it was clear that Carey operated with a team of leaders, rather than a single leader.

My role has been to help the church find its voice, and to recast vision for the second era at Carey. After dreaming together, the

Carey 2014 vision was birthed. Much has been achieved. A 55-acre site has been purchased on which to build a new campus. Plans for the new school and church are well advanced. It should commence in 2014. In addition, the foundations for the new community centre are due to be laid within a few months. The church has relocated to a larger auditorium on the campus to house the growing congregation. The youth group usually has over 200 teenagers in attendance, and also runs a night-time service at which budding preachers develop their skills, and fledgling worship leaders find wings. The church also runs an effective ministry in the local prison, and partners together with several schools in developing countries to enhance their work and mission. There is much energy and optimism. While people are talking about the success of the 2014 vision, some of us have started to talk about 'Carey 2019', and what the third stage in our development might mean.

Carey is undoubtedly a success story, but it is a success achieved because of the commitment and sacrifice of a range of ordinary people who continue to be willing to obey the call of God. They were blessed by a wonderful vision-caster in their opening decade, but have always known that if their vision is to be realized, they have to exercise their own version of quiet leadership. And exercise it they have . . .

Each time I walk on the campus, I am struck by its energy and life. I marvel at the multi-million-dollar facilities. I also remind myself that this was achieved by twenty-five ordinary twenty-somethings, who stayed true to their vision. They adopted an ambitious dream, and by systematically putting one foot in front of the next, they have achieved more than they dreamt would be possible. In closing this book it only remains for me to say that I am convinced that quiet leaders around the world, by staying true to their dreams, and by persistently and tenaciously placing one foot in front of the next, can do the same. Perhaps you are one of them . . .

References

Adair, John. *Inspiring Leaders: Learning from Great Leaders* (London: Thorogood, 2002).

Allender, Dan B. *Leading with a Limp: Turning Your Struggles into Strengths* (Colorado Springs: WaterBrook, 2006).

Andrews, Dave. *People of Compassion* (Blackburn, VIC: TEAR Australia, 2008).

Badaracco Jr., Joseph L. *Leading Quietly: An Unorthodox Guide to Doing the Right Thing* (Boston: Harvard Business School, 2002).

Banks, Robert and Bernice M. Ledbetter. *Reviewing Leadership: A Christian Evaluation of Current Approaches* (Grand Rapids: Baker, 2004).

Barna, George. *A Fish Out of Water: 9 Strategies to Maximize Your God-Given Leadership Potential* (Brentwood: Integrity, 2002).

Brueggeman, Walter. *Spirituality of the Psalms* (Minneapolis: Fortress, 2002).

Callaghan, Gregg. '10 Questions – Body Language Expert David Alssema'. *The Australian* (2 April 2011).

Chesterton, G.K. *What's Wrong with the World* (London: Cassell, 1910).

Cooperrider, D.L. 'The Child as Agent of Inquiry'. *Organizational Development Practitioner* 28 (1996): pp. 5–11.

Covey, Stephen R. *The Seven Habits of Highly Effective People: Restoring the Character Ethic* (London: Simon & Schuster, 1989).

Culbertson, Philip. *Caring for God's People: Counseling and Christian Wholeness* (Minneapolis: Fortress, 2000).

Dawkins, Richard. *The God Delusion* (Boston: Houghton Mifflin, 2006).

Dennison, Justin. *Team Ministry: A Blueprint for Christian Leadership* (London: Hodder & Stoughton, 1997).

Evans, Mary. 'The Powerless Leader: A Biblical Ideal or a Contradiction in Terms?' Pages 78–92 in *On Eagles' Wings: An Exploration of Strength in the Midst of Weakness* (ed. Michael Parsons and David J. Cohen; Eugene: Wipf & Stock, 2008).

Frost, Robert and Edward Connery Lathem. *The Poetry of Robert Frost* (New York: Henry Holt, 1969).

Fryling, Robert A. *The Leadership Ellipse: Shaping How We Lead by Who We Are* (Downers Grove: InterVarsity Press, 2010).

Greenleaf, Robert K. *Servant Leadership: A Journey into the Nature of Legitimate Power and Greatness* (New York: Paulist Press, 1977).

Grenz, Stanley J. *Revisioning Evangelical Theology: A Fresh Agenda for the Twenty First Century* (Downers Grove: InterVarsity Press, 1993).

_____. *The Moral Quest: Foundations of Christian Ethics* (Downers Grove: InterVarsity Press, 1997).

_____. *The Social God and the Relational Self: A Trinitarian Theology of the Imago Dei* (Louisville: Westminster John Knox Press, 2001).

Grenz, Stanley J. and John R. Franke. *Beyond Foundationalism: Shaping Theology in a Postmodern Context* (Louisville: Westminster John Knox Press, 2001).

Harris, Brian. 'When Faith Is the Problem'. *The Advocate* 4 (April 2007).

_____. *The Theological Method of Stanley J. Grenz: Constructing Evangelical Theology from Scripture, Tradition and Culture* (Lewiston: Edwin Mellen Press, 2011).

Harris, Sam. *Letters to a Christian Nation* (New York: Random, 2006).

Hitchens, Christopher. *God Is Not Great: How Religion Poisons Everything* (New York: Twelve, 2007).

The Holy Bible: New International Version. International Bible Society, 1984.

Hybels, Bill. *Courageous Leadership* (Grand Rapids: Zondervan, 2002).

_____. *Axiom: Powerful Leadership Proverbs* (Grand Rapids: Zondervan, 2008).

Jamieson, Alan. *A Churchless Faith: Faith Journeys Beyond Evangelical, Pentecostal and Charismatic Churches* (Wellington: Philip Garside Publishing, 2000).

References

Kinnaman, David and Gabe Lyons. *Unchristian: What a New Generation Really Thinks About Christianity . . . And Why It Matters* (Grand Rapids: Baker, 2007).

Kretzmann, John P. and John McKnight. *Building Communities from the Inside Out: A Path toward Finding and Mobilizing a Community's Assets* (Evanston: Asset-Based Community Development Institute, 1993).

Kuhn, Thomas. *The Structure of Scientific Revolutions* (Chicago: University of Chicago Press, 1962).

Leas, Speed B. *Discover Your Conflict Management Style* (Herndon, VA: Alban, 1997).

Lencioni, Patrick. *The Five Dysfunctions of a Team* (San Francisco: Jossey-Bass, 2002).

Lovin, Robin W. *Christian Ethics: An Essential Guide* (Nashville: Abingdon, 2000).

Ludema, James. 'From Deficit Discourse to Vocabularies of Hope: The Power of Appreciation'. Ch. 29 in *Appreciative Inquiry: An Emerging Direction for Organization Development* (ed. D.L. Cooperrider, Peter F. Sorensen Jr., Therese F. Yaeger and Diana Whitney; Champaign, IL: Stripes, 2001).

Maloney, H.N. *Living with Paradox: Religious Leadership and the Genius of Double Vision* (San Francisco: Jossey-Bass, 1998).

Maxwell, John C. *Developing the Leader within You* (Nashville: Thomas Nelson, 1993).

_____. *The 21 Irrefutable Laws of Leadership: Follow Them and People Will Follow You* (Nashville: Thomas Nelson, 1998).

_____. *The 21 Indispensible Qualities of a Leader: Becoming the Person Others Will Want to Follow* (Nashville: Thomas Nelson, 1999).

McKnight, Scot. *The Jesus Creed: Loving God, Loving Others* (Brewster: Paraclete Press, 2004).

Moltmann, Jürgen. *Theology of Hope: On the Ground and the Implications of a Christian Eschatology* (trans. James W. Leitch; London: SCM, 1967).

_____. *The Experiment Hope* (ed. and trans. M. Douglas Meeks. London: SCM, 1975).

Murray, Stuart. *Church after Christendom* (Carlisle: Paternoster, 2004).

_____. *Post-Christendom* (Carlisle: Paternoster, 2004).

Nelson, Alan and Stan Toler. *The Five Secrets to Becoming a Leader* (Ventura: Regal, 2002).

Noll, Mark A., ed. *The Princeton Theology 1812-1921: Scripture, Science, and Theological Method from Archibald Alexander to Benjamin Breckinridge Warfield* (Grand Rapids: Baker, 1983, reprinted 2001).

Nouwen, H. *The Wounded Healer* (New York: Doubleday, 1972).

Peck, M. Scott. *The Road Less Traveled: A New Psychology of Love, Traditional Values and Spiritual Growth* (New York: Simon & Schuster, 1978).

Peters, Thomas J. and Robert H. Waterman Jr. *In Search of Excellence: Lessons from America's Best-Run Companies* (Sydney: Harper & Row, 1982).

Placher, William C., ed. *Callings: Twenty Centuries of Christian Wisdom on Vocation* (Grand Rapids: Eerdmans, 2005).

Powell, Mark Allan. *What Do They Hear? Bridging the Gap Between Pulpit and Pew* (Nashville: Abingdon, 2007).

Scazzero, Peter. *Emotionally Healthy Spirituality* (Nashville: Thomas Nelson, 2006).

Schmidt, Alvin J. *Under the Influence: How Christianity Transformed Culture* (Grand Rapids: Zondervan, 2001).

Snow, Luther K. *The Power of Asset Mapping: How Your Congregation Can Act on Its Gifts* (Herndon: Alban Institute, 2004).

Stoddard, David A. and Robert J. Tamasy. *The Heart of Mentoring: Ten Proven Principles for Developing People to Their Fullest Potential* (Colorado Springs: Navpress, 2003).

Strom, Mark. *Arts of the Wise Leader* (Sydney: Sophos, 2007).

Sweetman, John. *A Theology of Christian Leadership: Follower-Focused Christian Leadership* (Brisbane: Malyon Centre for Christian Leadership, Undated).

Thomson, Joe C. 'Of Humans and Humanity'. *Time* (14 March 2011): p. 2.

Tidball, Derek. *Builders and Fools: Leadership the Bible Way* (Leicester: Inter-Varsity Press, 1999).

Wallis, Jim. *The Call to Conversion* (Herts: Lion, 1981).

Endnotes

1. The Tortoise Usually Wins: The Theory of Quiet Leadership

[1] Joseph L. Badaracco Jr., *Leading Quietly: An Unorthodox Guide to Doing the Right Thing* (Boston: Harvard Business School, 2002), p. 1.

[2] Badaracco, *Leading Quietly*, pp. 1–2.

[3] See, for example, John C. Maxwell, *The 21 Irrefutable Laws of Leadership: Follow Them and People Will Follow You* (Nashville: Thomas Nelson, 1998); John C. Maxwell, *The 21 Indispensible Qualities of a Leader: Becoming the Person Others Will Want to Follow* (Nashville: Thomas Nelson, 1999).

[4] Mark Strom, *Arts of the Wise Leader* (Sydney: Sophos, 2007), p. 49.

[5] Banks and Ledbetter embark on a helpful exploration of the emphases and implications of different approaches. Robert Banks and Bernice M. Ledbetter, *Reviewing Leadership: A Christian Evaluation of Current Approaches* (Grand Rapids: Baker, 2004).

[6] It's a book well worth reading. Dan B. Allender, *Leading with a Limp: Turning Your Struggles into Strengths* (Colorado Springs: WaterBrook, 2006).

[7] H.N. Maloney, *Living with Paradox: Religious Leadership and the Genius of Double Vision* (San Francisco: Jossey-Bass, 1998), p. xiv.

[8] Gen. 2:7

[9] Robert Frost and Edward Connery Lathem, *The Poetry of Robert Frost* (New York: Henry Holt, 1969), p. 224.

2. Servant, Shepherd and Steward: A Theology of Quiet Leadership

[1] I use the term 'models' (plural) intentionally, as the Bible offers many portraits of leadership. They are richly nuanced, and cannot be neatly reduced into one tidy model, though basic themes recur repeatedly (such as servant leadership).

[2] Robert K. Greenleaf, *Servant Leadership: A Journey into the Nature of Legitimate Power and Greatness* (New York: Paulist Press, 1977), p. 8.

[3] 1 Tim. 5:22 (New Living Translation)

[4] Phil. 1:1

[5] Mark 2:27

[6] Gen. 12:1–3

[7] Mary Evans, 'The Powerless Leader: A Biblical Ideal or a Contradiction in Terms?', in *On Eagles' Wings: An Exploration of Strength in the Midst of Weakness* (ed. Michael Parsons and David J. Cohen; Eugene: Wipf & Stock, 2008), p. 83.

[8] Some might argue that it is God-focused, but beware of leadership theories that use the name of God to justify practices that exploit others. It's a sure sign of toxic faith. Jesus was content to offer John 13:35 as a sign: 'By this all men will know that you are my disciples, if you have love one for another.'

[9] John Sweetman, *A Theology of Christian Leadership: Follower-Focused Christian Leadership* (Brisbane: Malyon Centre for Christian Leadership, Undated).

[10] Derek Tidball, *Builders and Fools: Leadership the Bible Way* (Leicester: InterVarsity Press, 1999), p. 148.

[11] 1 Sam. 17:34–6

[12] John 10:4

[13] See for example Luke 12:42–8 and Matt. 25:14–30.

[14] Luther K. Snow, *The Power of Asset Mapping: How Your Congregation Can Act on Its Gifts* (Herndon: Alban Institute, 2004).

[15] John P. Kretzmann and John McKnight, *Building Communities from the inside Out: A Path toward Finding and Mobilizing a Community's Assets* (Evanston: Asset-Based Community Development Institute, 1993). Cited in Snow, *Power*, p. 5.

[16] Derek Tidball, *Builders and Fools: Leadership the Bible Way* (Leicester: Inter-Varsity Press, 1999).

3. Becoming and Doing: Ethics and Virtues which Shape Quiet Leaders

1 Exod. 20:1–17
2 Robin W. Lovin, *Christian Ethics: An Essential Guide* (Nashville: Abingdon, 2000), p. 61.
3 This is an edited version of part of the T.B. Maston Lecture I delivered at Carson Newman College, East Tennessee, on 4 April 2011.
4 Stanley J. Grenz, *The Moral Quest: Foundations of Christian Ethics* (Downers Grove: InterVarsity Press, 1997), p. 31.
5 This claim is made in an interview with body-language specialist, David Alssema. Gregg Callaghan, '10 Questions – Body Language Expert David Alssema', *The Australian* (2 April 2011).
6 In public domain.
7 Gen. 1:27
8 See for example, Joseph L. Badaracco Jr., *Leading Quietly: An Unorthodox Guide to Doing the Right Thing* (Boston: Harvard Business School, 2002).
9 Badaracco, *Leading Quietly*, p. 173.
10 Badaracco, *Leading Quietly*, p. 174.
11 Badaracco, *Leading Quietly*, p. 19.
12 Badaracco, *Leading Quietly*, p. 171.
13 Badaracco, *Leading Quietly*, p. 172.
14 Badaracco, *Leading Quietly*, p. 144.
15 Philip Culbertson, *Caring for God's People: Counseling and Christian Wholeness* (Minneapolis: Fortress, 2000), p. 14.
16 Gen. 2:18
17 Eph. 3:18
18 Mark Strom, *Arts of the Wise Leader* (Sydney: Sophos, 2007), pp. 36–7.
19 Mark Allan Powell, *What Do They Hear? Bridging the Gap between Pulpit and Pew* (Nashville: Abingdon, 2007).

4. Discovering Your Voice: The Journey of Quiet Leadership

1 Attributed to Adam Kahane and cited in Strom, *Arts of the Wise Leader*, p. 64.

[2] William C. Placher, ed. *Callings: Twenty Centuries of Christian Wisdom on Vocation* (Grand Rapids: Eerdmans, 2005), p. 2.

[3] The approach was often linked to what is known as the Princeton Theology. For an exploration of the topic see Mark A. Noll, ed. *The Princeton Theology 1812-1921: Scripture, Science, and Theological Method from Archibald Alexander to Benjamin Breckinridge Warfield* (Grand Rapids: Baker, 1983; reprint, 2001).

[4] For a helpful introduction to this topic, with a special focus on the relevance of narrative theory to counseling situations, see Philip Culbertson, *Caring for God's People: Counseling and Christian Wholeness* (Minneapolis: Fortress, 2000), pp. 44–72.

[5] M. Scott Peck, *The Road Less Traveled: A New Psychology of Love, Traditional Values and Spiritual Growth* (New York: Simon and Schuster, 1978), p. 15.

[6] For a helpful and accessible introduction to psalms of orientation, disorientation and reorientation, see Walter Brueggeman, *Spirituality of the Psalms* (Minneapolis: Fortress, 2002).

[7] H. Nouwen, *The Wounded Healer* (New York: Doubleday, 1972).

[8] Ps. 150:6

[9] Robert A. Fryling, *The Leadership Ellipse: Shaping How We Lead by Who We Are* (Downers Grove: InterVarsity Press, 2010), p. 15.

[10] Culbertson, *Caring for God's People*, p. 58.

5. Challenging Our Excuses: Quiet Leadership and Character Development

[1] Scot McKnight, *The Jesus Creed: Loving God, Loving Others* (Brewster: Paraclete Press, 2004).

[2] Peter Scazzero, *Emotionally Healthy Spirituality* (Nashville: Thomas Nelson, 2006), pp. 23–37.

[3] The remaining part of this section is a lightly edited version of the lunchtime T.B. Maston Lecture I delivered at Carson Newman College in East Tennessee. Brian Harris, *The Theological Method of Stanley J. Grenz: Constructing Evangelical Theology from Scripture, Tradition and Culture* (Lewiston: Edwin Mellen Press, 2011).

[4] Joe C. Thomson, 'Of Humans and Humanity', *Time* (14 March 2011), p. 2.

[5] Christopher Hitchens, *God Is Not Great: How Religion Poisons Everything* (New York: Twelve, 2007).

6 Two other popular examples are Richard Dawkins, *The God Delusion* (Boston: Houghton Mifflin, 2006); and Sam Harris, *Letters to a Christian Nation* (New York: Random, 2006).

7 G.K. Chesterton, *What's Wrong with the World* (London: Cassell, 1910), p. 48.

8 David Kinnaman and Gabe Lyons, *Unchristian: What a New Generation Really Thinks About Christianity . . . And Why It Matters* (Grand Rapids: Baker, 2007).

9 For a discussion of and rationale for the conclusion that we live in a 'post-Christendom' era, see Stuart Murray, *Church after Christendom* (Carlisle: Paternoster, 2004); Stuart Murray, *Post-Christendom* (Carlisle: Paternoster, 2004).

10 For a very different (and far more positive) interpretation of the churches contribution to society, see Alvin J. Schmidt, *Under the Influence: How Christianity Transformed Culture* (Grand Rapids: Zondervan, 2001).

11 A simple but thought provoking introduction to the topic is found in Dave Andrews, *People of Compassion* (Blackburn, VIC: TEAR Australia, 2008).

12 While it can be argued that we should distinguish between the Christ story and the history of the churches founded as a result of that story, in practice this is difficult to do. It is however true that the Christ story could (and probably should) serve as the filter to determine the faithfulness or otherwise of the churches formed to their mandate to serve as Christ's body on earth.

13 So, for example, Jim Wallis, speaking of the mixed legacy of Evangelicalism, laments, 'Evangelicals in this century have a history of going along with the culture on the big issues and taking their stand on the smaller issues. That has been one of the serious problems of evangelical religion. Today, many evangelicals no longer just acquiesce to the culture on the larger economic and political issues, but actively promote the culture's worst values on these matters.' Jim Wallis, *The Call to Conversion* (Herts: Lion, 1981), p. 25.

14 The following three paragraphs are a slightly modified form of part of a brief newspaper article I wrote in 2007. Brian Harris, 'When Faith Is the Problem', *The Advocate* (April 2007).

15 See for example Stanley J. Grenz, *Revisioning Evangelical Theology: A Fresh Agenda for the Twenty First Century* (Downers Grove: InterVarsity Press, 1993); Stanley J. Grenz and John R. Franke, *Beyond Foundationalism*:

Shaping Theology in a Postmodern Context (Louisville: Westminster John Knox Press, 2001).

16 Stanley J. Grenz, *The Social God and the Relational Self: A Trinitarian Theology of the Imago Dei* (Louisville: Westminster John Knox Press, 2001).

6. Results Matter: Quiet Leadership and Optimizing Outputs

1 Patrick Lencioni, *The Five Dysfunctions of a Team* (San Francisco: Jossey-Bass, 2002), p. 219.

2 Hitler was undoubtedly a leader, but he was not a good leader as he moved things in a destructive direction. Defining what constitutes a positive direction can be difficult, but in a Christian context would include moving in a direction consistent with the eschatological vision found within Scripture.

3 D.L. Cooperrider, 'The Child as Agent of Inquiry', *Organizational Development Practitioner* 28 (1996): p. 11.

4 For an exploration of the concept, see James Ludema, 'From Deficit Discourse to Vocabularies of Hope: The Power of Appreciation', in *Appreciative Inquiry: An Emerging Direction for Organization Development* (ed. D.L. Cooperrider et al.; Champaign, IL: Stripes, 2001).

5 See Rev. 21.

6 See for example Jürgen Moltmann, *Theology of Hope: On the Ground and the Implications of a Christian Eschatology* (trans. James W. Leitch; London: SCM, 1967); Jürgen Moltmann, *The Experiment Hope* (trans. M. Douglas Meeks; London: SCM, 1975).

7 Cooperrider, 'The Child as Agent of Inquiry', pp. 5–11.

8 Thomas J. Peters and Robert H. Waterman Jr., *In Search of Excellence: Lessons from America's Best-Run Companies* (Sydney: Harper & Row, 1982), p. 238.

9 Peters and Waterman, *In Search of Excellence*, p. 240.

10 Peters and Waterman, *In Search of Excellence*, pp. 260–62.

7. Casting Vision, Reshaping Paradigms: Quiet Leaders as Change Agents

1 Which, as Stephen Covey notes, is one of the habits of highly effective people. He lists it at no. 3, after the related habits of being proactive and beginning with the end in mind. Stephen R. Covey, *The Seven Habits of Highly Effective People: Restoring the Character Ethic* (London: Simon & Schuster, 1989), pp. 63–182.

2 Thomas Kuhn, *The Structure of Scientific Revolutions* (Chicago: University of Chicago Press, 1962).

3 Acts 1:6

4 Bill Hybels, *Courageous Leadership* (Grand Rapids: Zondervan, 2002), p. 32.

5 Alan Nelson and Stan Toler, *The Five Secrets to Becoming a Leader* (Ventura: Regal, 2002), p. 36.

6 John C. Maxwell. *The 21 Indispensible Qualities of a Leader: Becoming the Person Others Will Want to Follow* (Nashville: Thomas Nelson, 1999).

7 John C. Maxwell, *Developing the Leader within You* (Nashville: Thomas Nelson, 1993), p. 141.

8 Covey, *Seven Habits*, p. 78.

9 Covey, *Seven Habits*, p. 99.

10 Maxwell, *Developing the Leader within You*, p. 146.

11 Hybels, *Courageous Leadership*, p. 51.

12 Hybels, *Courageous Leadership*, p. 52.

8. What Others Become: Quiet Leadership and Helping Others Shine

1 I'm using the ideas in a slightly different way from Stoddard and Tamasy, but their alliteration sparked my thinking in this area. David A. Stoddard and Robert J. Tamasy, *The Heart of Mentoring: Ten Proven Principles for Developing People to Their Fullest Potential* (Colorado Springs: Navpress, 2003), p. 25.

2 Gen. 3:17–19

3 Gen. 1:28–31

4 Gen. 2:19–20

5 Col. 3:17

6 See for example Luke 9:28–36.

7   Acts 1:15
8   John 6:14,66
9   Gen. 2:7
10 Bill Hybels, *Axiom: Powerful Leadership Proverbs* (Grand Rapids: Zondervan, 2008), axiom 45.
11 Prov. 17:22 (NRSV).

9. From Leadership to Leaderships: Getting Teams to Work in the Same Direction

1 Mark Strom, *Arts of the Wise Leader* (Sydney: Sophos, 2007), p. 73.
2 Patrick Lencioni, *The Five Dysfunctions of a Team* (San Francisco: Jossey-Bass, 2002).

10. Beyond Dreaming: Quiet Leadership and the Management/Leadership Juggle

1 Robert Banks and Bernice M. Ledbetter, *Reviewing Leadership: A Christian Evaluation of Current Approaches* (Grand Rapids: Baker, 2004), p. 17.
2 Stephen R. Covey, *The Seven Habits of Highly Effective People: Restoring the Character Ethic* (London: Simon & Schuster, 1989), p. 171.
3 Bill Hybels, *Axiom: Powerful Leadership Proverbs* (Grand Rapids: Zondervan, 2008), pp. 142–4.
4 Justin Dennison, *Team Ministry: A Blueprint for Christian Leadership* (London: Hodder & Stoughton, 1997), pp. 118–30.
5 Eph. 4:15
6 Leas, Speed B. *Discover Your Conflict Management Style* (Herndon, VA: Alban, 1997).
7 Matt. 6:33

11. Some Tortoise Triumphs: Quiet Leadership in Practice

1 For the technically minded, remoteness is defined as the distance between a city of one million people or more and another city of at least a million people. By that definition, Auckland's closest neighbour

is Sydney, 2168.9km away, while Perth comes a close second with 2139 km separating it and Adelaide.

2 Alan Jamieson, *A Churchless Faith: Faith Journeys Beyond Evangelical, Pentecostal and Charismatic Churches* (Wellington: Philip Garside Publishing, 2000).

Paternoster:
thinking faith

We trust you enjoyed reading this book
from Paternoster. If you want to be informed
of any new titles from this author and other
releases you can sign up to the Paternoster
newsletter by contacting us:

By Post:
Paternoster
52 Presley Way
Crownhill
Milton Keynes
MK8 0ES

E-mail
paternoster@authenticmedia.co.uk

Follow us: